Y0-BZU-287

THE
RACING RULES
OF SAILING

for 2009–2012

Including US SAILING Prescriptions

www.ussailing.org

United States Sailing Association
15 Maritime Drive, Post Office Box 1260
Portsmouth, RI 02871

The Racing Rules of Sailing for 2009–2012
Including US SAILING Prescriptions

ISBN: 978-0-9794677-5-2

Issue Date: November 2008
Frequency: Quadrennially
Authorizing Organization: US SAILING
Post Office Box 1260, 15 Maritime Drive
Portsmouth, RI 02871
Issue Number: Issue No. 1

A Note from US SAILING's President

The Racing Rules of Sailing for 2009-2012 take effect worldwide on January 1, 2009. There are some important changes in this edition, especially to rules that apply to marks and obstructions. Racing sailors, particularly those who drive the boat, need to know the rights and obligations of their boat in any situation, and be able to apply them without hesitation. As with each new edition, it is important to carefully study the rules that apply between boats on the race course — the definitions and the rules of Part 1 and Part 2. In this edition, these rules will look familiar to sailors who raced under the previous editions published since 1997. In spite of the similarities, many volunteers from around the world have spent a lot of time working to make the new edition of the rules clearer and simpler.

It has not always been the case that sailors raced under a universally accepted set of racing rules. Prior to 1960, the basic racing rules varied from country to country, and even from club to club, with right of way adopted from the maritime rules of the road. Over the years, US SAILING has played a large role in the development of the international rules we use today.

In 1949, US SAILING (formerly NAYRU) officially adopted a code of racing rules developed over the previous fifteen years by Harold S. Vanderbilt, a member of our Racing Rules and Appeals Committees. The Vanderbilt rules were tested extensively in North America and beginning in 1958, in Scandinavia. Bob Bavier and F. Gregg Bemis, our delegates to ISAF (formerly IYRU), worked to adapt the NAYRU rules for international use. Finally, in 1960, sailors had a single set of simplified rules worldwide. Since then, US SAILING and its volunteers, especially Harman Hawkins, Bill Bentsen and Dick Rose, continued to make significant contributions to the racing rules that we use around the world today.

Good sailing,
Jim Capron, President

Note: In considering rules situations, one knot is equal to 1.688 feet per second, and the time in seconds to travel one hull length is equal to: (hull length in feet / boat speed in knots) x 0.5925.

Contents

Foreword

This 2009-2012 edition of *The Racing Rules of Sailing* was produced after four years of careful review of the 2005-2008 rulebook by the International Sailing Federation (ISAF). Significant changes were made in the rules and definitions that apply at marks and obstructions. These include new rules 18, 19 and 20 and the new definitions *Mark-Room*, *Zone* and *Fetching* as well as the definitions *Clear Astern*, *Clear Ahead*, *Overlap* and *Obstruction*. Marginal markings in Parts 1-7 and Definitions indicate these and other noteworthy changes.

In addition to the ISAF rules, this rulebook contains 'prescriptions' adopted by US SAILING for events held in the United States. These rules appear throughout this book in ***bold italics***. They do not apply when racing at a regatta in another country; in that case, refer to the prescriptions in that country's rulebook.

Helpful information about the rules is available on the Racing Rules page at the US SAILING website. You can get there by going to www.ussailing.org/rules. This page has links to publications and materials referenced in this book, including:

- *The Case Book*
- *The Call Book for Match Racing*
- *The Call Book for Team Racing*
- the ISAF Regulations, including the ISAF Eligibility, Advertising, Anti-Doping and Sailor Classification Codes
- the government right-of-way rules referred to in the preamble to Part 2, and
- the publications referred to in the prescriptions to rule 40, 82 and G2 and in the US SAILING Notes in Appendices A, *BB* and L.

The Racing Rules page also contains links to other educational materials for both beginning and experienced sailors.

Most of the rule changes in this book are the result of suggestions from competitors and race officials. The US SAILING Racing Rules Committee welcomes your ideas on how to improve the racing rules for the next rulebook. Please e-mail comments and proposals to rules@ussailing.org, or mail them to the US SAILING Racing Rules Committee, P. O. Box 1260, Portsmouth, RI 02871-0907.

David Dellenbaugh, Chairman

US SAILING Racing Rules Committee: Ben Altman, Arthur Engel, Scott Ikle, Matthew Knowles, Rob Overton, Dick Rose, Mary Savage

Introduction

The Racing Rules of Sailing includes two main sections. The first, Parts 1–7, contains rules that affect all competitors. The second, Appendices A–P, provides details of rules, rules that apply to particular kinds of racing, and rules that affect only a small number of competitors or officials.

Revision The racing rules are revised and published every four years by the International Sailing Federation (ISAF), the international authority for the sport. This edition becomes effective on 1 January 2009 except that for an event beginning in 2008 the date may be postponed by the notice of race and sailing instructions. Marginal markings indicate important changes to Parts 1–7 and the Definitions of the 2005–2008 edition. No changes are contemplated before 2013, but any changes determined to be urgent before then will be announced through national authorities and posted on the ISAF website (www.sailing.org).

ISAF Codes The ISAF Eligibility, Advertising, Anti-Doping and Sailor Classification Codes (Regulations 19, 20, 21 and 22) are referred to in the definition *Rule* but are not included in this book because they can be changed at any time. The most recent versions of the codes are available on the ISAF website; new versions will be announced through national authorities.

Cases and Calls The ISAF publishes interpretations of the racing rules in *The Case Book for 2009–2012* and recognizes them as authoritative interpretations and explanations of the rules. It also publishes *The Call Book for Match Racing for 2009–2012* and *The Call Book for Team Racing for 2009–2012*, and it recognizes them as authoritative only for umpired match or team racing. These publications are available on the ISAF website.

Terminology A term used in the sense stated in the Definitions is printed in *italics* or, in preambles, in ***bold italics*** (for example, *racing* and ***racing***). 'Racing rule' means a rule in *The Racing Rules of Sailing*. 'Boat' means a sailboat and the crew on board. 'Race committee' includes any person or committee performing a race committee function. A 'change' to a *rule* includes an addition to it or deletion of all or part of it. 'National authority' means an ISAF member national authority. Other words and terms are used in the sense ordinarily understood in nautical or general use.

Appendices When the rules of an appendix apply, they take precedence over any conflicting rules in Parts 1–7 and the Definitions. Each appendix is identified by a letter. A reference to a rule in an appendix will contain the letter and the rule number (for example, 'rule A1'). There is no Appendix I or O.

Changes to the Rules The prescriptions of a national authority, class rules or the sailing instructions may change a racing rule only as permitted in rule 86.

Changes to National Authority Prescriptions A national authority may restrict changes to its prescriptions as provided in rule 88.2.

Prescriptions US SAILING prescriptions are printed in bold italics, except Appendices BB, F and S. Those three appendices are US SAILING prescriptions. There is no Appendix Q or R.

Equal Opportunity

As the national authority for the sport of sailing, US SAILING is committed to providing an equal opportunity to all sailors to participate in the sport of sailing.

Basic Principle

Sportsmanship and the Rules

Competitors in the sport of sailing are governed by a body of *rules* that they are expected to follow and enforce. A fundamental principle of sportsmanship is that when competitors break a *rule* they will promptly take a penalty, which may be to retire.

Part 1 — Fundamental Rules

1 SAFETY

1.1 Helping Those in Danger

A boat or competitor shall give all possible help to any person or vessel in danger.

1.2 Life-Saving Equipment and Personal Flotation Devices

A boat shall carry adequate life-saving equipment for all persons on board, including one item ready for immediate use, unless her class rules make some other provision. Each competitor is individually responsible for wearing a personal flotation device adequate for the conditions.

2 FAIR SAILING

A boat and her owner shall compete in compliance with recognized principles of sportsmanship and fair play. A boat may be penalized under this rule only if it is clearly established that these principles have been violated. A disqualification under this rule shall not be excluded from the boat's series score.

3 ACCEPTANCE OF THE RULES

By participating in a race conducted under these racing rules, each competitor and boat owner agrees

(a) to be governed by the *rules*;

(b) to accept the penalties imposed and other action taken under the *rules*, subject to the appeal and review procedures provided in them, as the final determination of any matter arising under the *rules*; and

(c) with respect to any such determination, not to resort to any court of law or tribunal.

4   **DECISION TO RACE**

The responsibility for a boat's decision to participate in a race or to continue *racing* is hers alone.

5   **ANTI-DOPING**

A competitor shall comply with the World Anti-Doping Code, the rules of the World Anti-Doping Agency, and ISAF Regulation 21, Anti-Doping Code. An alleged or actual breach of this rule shall be dealt with under Regulation 21. It shall not be grounds for a *protest* and rule 63.1 does not apply.

Part 2 — When Boats Meet

*The rules of Part 2 apply between boats that are sailing in or near the racing area and intend to **race**, are **racing**, or have been **racing**. However, a boat not **racing** shall not be penalized for breaking one of these rules, except rule 23.1.*

When a boat sailing under these rules meets a vessel that is not, she shall comply with the International Regulations for Preventing Collisions at Sea (IRPCAS) *or government right-of-way rules. If the sailing instructions so state, the rules of Part 2 are replaced by the right-of-way rules of the* IRPCAS *or by government right-of-way rules.*

Section A — Right of Way

*A boat has right of way when another boat is required to **keep clear** of her. However, some rules in Sections B, C and D limit the actions of a right-of-way boat.*

10 ON OPPOSITE TACKS

When boats are on opposite *tacks*, a *port-tack* boat shall *keep clear* of a *starboard-tack* boat.

11 ON THE SAME TACK, OVERLAPPED

When boats are on the same *tack* and *overlapped*, a *windward* boat shall *keep clear* of a *leeward* boat.

12 ON THE SAME TACK, NOT OVERLAPPED

When boats are on the same *tack* and not *overlapped*, a boat *clear astern* shall *keep clear* of a boat *clear ahead*.

13 WHILE TACKING

After a boat passes head to wind, she shall *keep clear* of other boats until she is on a close-hauled course. During that time rules 10, 11 and 12 do not apply. If two boats are subject to this rule at the same time, the one on the other's port side or the one astern shall *keep clear*.

Section B — General Limitations

14   AVOIDING CONTACT

A boat shall avoid contact with another boat if reasonably possible. However, a right-of-way boat or one entitled to *room* or *mark-room*

(a)   need not act to avoid contact until it is clear that the other boat is not *keeping clear* or giving *room* or *mark-room*, and

(b)   shall not be penalized under this rule unless there is contact that causes damage or injury.

15   ACQUIRING RIGHT OF WAY

When a boat acquires right of way, she shall initially give the other boat *room* to *keep clear*, unless she acquires right of way because of the other boat's actions.

16   CHANGING COURSE

16.1 When a right-of-way boat changes course, she shall give the other boat *room* to *keep clear*.

16.2 In addition, when after the starting signal a *port-tack* boat is *keeping clear* by sailing to pass astern of a *starboard-tack* boat, the *starboard-tack* boat shall not change course if as a result the *port-tack* boat would immediately need to change course to continue *keeping clear*.

17   ON THE SAME TACK; PROPER COURSE

If a boat *clear astern* becomes *overlapped* within two of her hull lengths to *leeward* of a boat on the same *tack*, she shall not sail above her *proper course* while they remain on the same *tack* and *overlapped* within that distance, unless in doing so she promptly sails astern of the other boat. This rule does not apply if the *overlap* begins while the *windward* boat is required by rule 13 to *keep clear*.

Section C — At Marks and Obstructions

*Section C rules do not apply at a starting **mark** surrounded by navigable water or at its anchor line from the time boats are approaching them to **start** until they have passed them. When rule 20 applies, rules 18 and 19 do not.*

18   MARK-ROOM

18.1   When Rule 18 Applies

Rule 18 applies between boats when they are required to leave a *mark* on the same side and at least one of them is in the *zone*. However, it does not apply

(a) between boats on opposite *tacks* on a beat to windward,

(b) between boats on opposite *tacks* when the *proper course* at the *mark* for one but not both of them is to tack,

(c) between a boat approaching a *mark* and one leaving it, or

(d) if the *mark* is a continuing *obstruction*, in which case rule 19 applies.

18.2   Giving Mark-Room

(a) When boats are *overlapped* the outside boat shall give the inside boat *mark-room*, unless rule 18.2(b) applies.

(b) If boats are *overlapped* when the first of them reaches the *zone*, the outside boat at that moment shall thereafter give the inside boat *mark-room*. If a boat is *clear ahead* when she reaches the *zone*, the boat *clear astern* at that moment shall thereafter give her *mark-room*.

(c) When a boat is required to give *mark-room* by rule 18.2(b), she shall continue to do so even if later an *overlap* is broken or a new *overlap* begins. However, if either boat passes head to wind or if the boat entitled to *mark-room* leaves the *zone*, rule 18.2(b) ceases to apply.

(d) If there is reasonable doubt that a boat obtained or broke an *overlap* in time, it shall be presumed that she did not.

(e) If a boat obtained an inside *overlap* from *clear astern* and, from the time the *overlap* began, the outside boat has been unable to give *mark-room*, she is not required to give it.

18.3 Tacking When Approaching a Mark

If two boats were approaching a *mark* on opposite *tacks* and one of them changes *tack*, and as a result is subject to rule 13 in the *zone* when the other is *fetching* the *mark*, rule 18.2 does not thereafter apply. The boat that changed *tack*

(a) shall not cause the other boat to sail above close-hauled to avoid her or prevent the other boat from passing the *mark* on the required side, and

(b) shall give *mark-room* if the other boat becomes *overlapped* inside her.

18.4 Gybing

When an inside *overlapped* right-of-way boat must gybe at a *mark* to sail her *proper course*, until she gybes she shall sail no farther from the *mark* than needed to sail that course. Rule 18.4 does not apply at a gate *mark*.

18.5 Exoneration

When a boat is taking *mark-room* to which she is entitled, she shall be exonerated

(a) if, as a result of the other boat failing to give her *mark-room*, she breaks a rule of Section A, or

(b) if, by rounding the *mark* on her *proper course*, she breaks a rule of Section A or rule 15 or 16.

19 ROOM TO PASS AN OBSTRUCTION

19.1 When Rule 19 Applies

Rule 19 applies between boats at an *obstruction* except when it is also a *mark* the boats are required to leave on the same side. However, at a continuing *obstruction*, rule 19 always applies and rule 18 does not.

19.2 Giving Room at an Obstruction

(a) A right-of-way boat may choose to pass an *obstruction* on either side.

(b) When boats are *overlapped*, the outside boat shall give the inside boat *room* between her and the *obstruction*, unless she has been unable to do so from the time the *overlap* began.

(c) While boats are passing a continuing *obstruction*, if a boat that was *clear astern* and required to *keep clear* becomes *overlapped* between the other boat and the *obstruction* and, at the moment the *overlap* begins, there is not *room* for her to pass between them, she is not entitled to *room* under rule 19.2(b). While the boats remain *overlapped*, she shall *keep clear* and rules 10 and 11 do not apply.

20 ROOM TO TACK AT AN OBSTRUCTION

20.1 Hailing and Responding

When approaching an *obstruction*, a boat sailing close-hauled or above may hail for *room* to tack and avoid another boat on the same *tack*. After a boat hails,

(a) she shall give the hailed boat time to respond;

(b) the hailed boat shall respond either by tacking as soon as possible, or by immediately replying 'You tack' and then giving the hailing boat *room* to tack and avoid her; and

(c) when the hailed boat responds, the hailing boat shall tack as soon as possible.

20.2 Exoneration

When a boat is taking *room* to which she is entitled under rule 20.1(b), she shall be exonerated if she breaks a rule of Section A or rule 15 or 16.

20.3 When Not to Hail

A boat shall not hail unless safety requires her to make a substantial course change to avoid the *obstruction*. Also, she shall not hail if the *obstruction* is a *mark* that the hailed boat is *fetching*.

Section D — Other Rules

When rule 21 or 22 applies between two boats, Section A rules do not.

21 STARTING ERRORS; TAKING PENALTIES; MOVING ASTERN

21.1 A boat sailing towards the pre-start side of the starting line or one of its extensions after her starting signal to *start* or to comply with rule 30.1 shall *keep clear* of a boat not doing so until she is completely on the prestart side.

21.2 A boat taking a penalty shall *keep clear* of one that is not.

21.3 A boat moving astern by backing a sail shall *keep clear* of one that is not.

22 CAPSIZED, ANCHORED OR AGROUND; RESCUING

If possible, a boat shall avoid a boat that is capsized or has not regained control after capsizing, is anchored or aground, or is trying to help a person or vessel in danger. A boat is capsized when her masthead is in the water.

23 INTERFERING WITH ANOTHER BOAT

23.1 If reasonably possible, a boat not *racing* shall not interfere with a boat that is *racing*.

23.2 Except when sailing her *proper course*, a boat shall not interfere with a boat taking a penalty or sailing on another leg.

Part 3 — Conduct of a Race

25 NOTICE OF RACE, SAILING INSTRUCTIONS AND SIGNALS

The notice of race and sailing instructions shall be made available to each boat before a race begins. The meanings of the visual and sound signals stated in Race Signals shall not be changed except under rule 86.1(b). The meanings of any other signals that may be used shall be stated in the sailing instructions.

26 STARTING RACES

Races shall be started by using the following signals. Times shall be taken from the visual signals; the absence of a sound signal shall be disregarded.

Signal	Flag and sound	Minutes before starting signal
Warning	Class flag; 1 sound	5*
Preparatory	P, I, Z, Z with I, or black flag; 1 sound	4
One-minute	Preparatory flag removed; 1 long sound	1
Starting	Class flag removed; 1 sound	0

* or as stated in the sailing instructions

The warning signal for each succeeding class shall be made with or after the starting signal of the preceding class.

27 OTHER RACE COMMITTEE ACTIONS BEFORE THE STARTING SIGNAL

27.1 No later than the warning signal, the race committee shall signal or otherwise designate the course to be sailed if the sailing instructions have not stated the course, and it may replace one course signal with another and signal that wearing personal flotation devices is required (display flag Y with one sound).

27.2 No later than the preparatory signal, the race committee may move a starting *mark*.

27.3 Before the starting signal, the race committee may for any reason *postpone* (display flag AP, AP over H, or AP over A, with two sounds) or *abandon* the race (display flag N over H, or N over A, with three sounds).

28 SAILING THE COURSE

28.1 A boat shall *start*, leave each *mark* on the required side in the correct order, and *finish*, so that a string representing her track after *starting* and until *finishing* would when drawn taut

(a) pass each *mark* on the required side,

(b) touch each rounding *mark*, and

(c) pass between the *marks* of a gate from the direction of the previous *mark*.

She may correct any errors to comply with this rule. After *finishing* she need not cross the finishing line completely.

28.2 A boat may leave on either side a *mark* that does not begin, bound or end the leg she is on. However, she shall leave a starting *mark* on the required side when she is approaching the starting line from its pre-start side to *start*.

29 RECALLS

29.1 Individual Recall

When at a boat's starting signal any part of her hull, crew or equipment is on the course side of the starting line or she must comply with rule 30.1, the race committee shall promptly display flag X with one sound. The flag shall be displayed until all such boats are completely on the pre-start side of the starting line or one of its extensions and have complied with rule 30.1 if it applies, but no later than four minutes after the starting signal or one minute before any later starting signal, whichever is earlier. If rule 30.3 applies this rule does not.

29.2 General Recall

When at the starting signal the race committee is unable to identify boats that are on the course side of the starting line or to which rule 30 applies, or there has been an error in the starting procedure, the race committee may signal a general recall (display the First Substitute with two sounds).

The warning signal for a new start for the recalled class shall be made one minute after the First Substitute is removed (one sound), and the starts for any succeeding classes shall follow the new start.

30   STARTING PENALTIES

30.1 I Flag Rule

If flag I has been displayed, and any part of a boat's hull, crew or equipment is on the course side of the starting line or one of its extensions during the last minute before her starting signal, she shall thereafter sail from the course side across an extension to the pre-start side before *starting*.

30.2 Z Flag Rule

If flag Z has been displayed, no part of a boat's hull, crew or equipment shall be in the triangle formed by the ends of the starting line and the first *mark* during the last minute before her starting signal. If a boat breaks this rule and is identified, she shall receive, without a hearing, a 20% Scoring Penalty calculated as stated in rule 44.3(c). She shall be penalized even if the race is restarted or resailed, but not if it is *postponed* or *abandoned* before the starting signal. If she is similarly identified during a subsequent attempt to start the same race, she shall receive an additional 20% Scoring Penalty.

30.3 Black Flag Rule

If a black flag has been displayed, no part of a boat's hull, crew or equipment shall be in the triangle formed by the ends of the starting line and the first *mark* during the last minute before her starting signal. If a boat breaks this rule and is identified, she shall be disqualified without a hearing, even if the race is restarted or resailed, but not if it is *postponed* or *abandoned* before the starting signal. If a general recall is signalled or the race is *abandoned* after the starting signal, the race committee shall display her sail number before the next warning signal for that race, and if the race is restarted or resailed she shall not sail in it. If she does so, her disqualification shall not be excluded in calculating her series score.

31 TOUCHING A MARK

While *racing*, a boat shall not touch a starting *mark* before *starting*, a *mark* that begins, bounds or ends the leg of the course on which she is sailing, or a finishing *mark* after *finishing*.

32 SHORTENING OR ABANDONING AFTER THE START

32.1 After the starting signal, the race committee may shorten the course (display flag S with two sounds) or *abandon* the race (display flag N, N over H, or N over A, with three sounds), as appropriate,

(a) because of an error in the starting procedure,

(b) because of foul weather,

(c) because of insufficient wind making it unlikely that any boat will *finish* within the time limit,

(d) because a *mark* is missing or out of position, or

(e) for any other reason directly affecting the safety or fairness of the competition,

or may shorten the course so that other scheduled races can be sailed. However, after one boat has sailed the course and *finished* within the time limit, if any, the race committee shall not *abandon* the race without considering the consequences for all boats in the race or series.

32.2 If the race committee signals a shortened course (displays flag S with two sounds), the finishing line shall be,

(a) at a rounding *mark*, between the *mark* and a staff displaying flag S;

(b) at a line boats are required to cross at the end of each lap, that line;

(c) at a gate, between the gate *marks*.

The shortened course shall be signalled before the first boat crosses the finishing line.

33 CHANGING THE NEXT LEG OF THE COURSE

The race committee may change a leg of the course that begins at a rounding *mark* or at a gate by changing the position of the next *mark* (or the finishing line) and signalling all boats before they begin the leg. The next *mark* need not be in position at that time.

(a) If the direction of the leg will be changed, the signal shall be the display of flag C with repetitive sounds and either

    (1) the new compass bearing or

    (2) a green triangular flag or board for a change to starboard or a red rectangular flag or board for a change to port.

(b) If the length of the leg will be changed, the signal shall be the display of flag C with repetitive sounds and a '−' if the length will be decreased or a '+' if it will be increased.

(c) Subsequent legs may be changed without further signalling to maintain the course shape.

34   MARK MISSING; *RACE COMMITTEE ABSENT*

If a *mark* is missing or out of position, the race committee shall, if possible,

(a) replace it in its correct position or substitute a new one of similar appearance, or

(b) substitute an object displaying flag M and make repetitive sound signals.

US SAILING prescribes that, if a finishing mark *is missing but another one remains in place, a boat shall* finish *as close to the remaining* mark *as practicable on a line extending from its required side at a 90° angle to the last leg. If a boat* finishes *when the race committee is absent, to be scored as* finishing *she shall note her finishing time and her finishing position in relation to any nearby boats and report them to the race committee as soon as reasonably possible.*

35   TIME LIMIT AND SCORES

If one boat sails the course as required by rule 28.1 and *finishes* within the time limit, if any, all boats that *finish* shall be scored according to their finishing places unless the race is *abandoned*. If no boat *finishes* within the time limit, the race committee shall *abandon* the race.

36   RACES RESTARTED OR RESAILED

If a race is restarted or resailed, a breach of a *rule*, other than rule 30.3, in the original race shall not prohibit a boat from competing or, except under rule 30.2, 30.3 or 69, cause her to be penalized.

Part 4 — Other Requirements When Racing

*Part 4 rules apply only to boats **racing**.*

40 PERSONAL FLOTATION DEVICES; *LIFE-SAVING EQUIPMENT*

When flag Y is displayed with one sound before or with the warning signal, competitors shall wear personal flotation devices, except briefly while changing or adjusting clothing or personal equipment. Wet suits and dry suits are not personal flotation devices.

US SAILING prescribes that every boat shall carry life-saving equipment conforming to government regulations that apply in the racing area. See www.ussailing.org/rules/pfd for more information.

41 OUTSIDE HELP

A boat shall not receive help from any outside source, except

(a) help for an ill or injured crew member;

(b) after a collision, help from the crew of the other boat to get clear;

(c) help in the form of information freely available to all boats;

(d) unsolicited information from a disinterested source, which may be another boat in the same race.

42 PROPULSION

42.1 Basic Rule

Except when permitted in rule 42.3 or 45, a boat shall compete by using only the wind and water to increase, maintain or decrease her speed. Her crew may adjust the trim of sails and hull, and perform other acts of seamanship, but shall not otherwise move their bodies to propel the boat.

42.2 Prohibited Actions

Without limiting the application of rule 42.1, these actions are prohibited:

(a) pumping: repeated fanning of any sail either by pulling in and releasing the sail or by vertical or athwartship body movement;

   (b) rocking: repeated rolling of the boat, induced by
      (1) body movement,
      (2) repeated adjustment of the sails or centreboard, or
      (3) steering;
   (c) ooching: sudden forward body movement, stopped abruptly;
   (d) sculling: repeated movement of the helm that is either forceful or that propels the boat forward or prevents her from moving astern;
   (e) repeated tacks or gybes unrelated to changes in the wind or to tactical considerations.

42.3 Exceptions

   (a) A boat may be rolled to facilitate steering.

   (b) A boat's crew may move their bodies to exaggerate the rolling that facilitates steering the boat through a tack or a gybe, provided that, just after the tack or gybe is completed, the boat's speed is not greater than it would have been in the absence of the tack or gybe.

   (c) Except on a beat to windward, when surfing (rapidly accelerating down the leeward side of a wave) or planing is possible, the boat's crew may pull the sheet and the guy controlling any sail in order to initiate surfing or planing, but only once for each wave or gust of wind.

   (d) When a boat is above a close-hauled course and either stationary or moving slowly, she may scull to turn to a close-hauled course.

   (e) A boat may reduce speed by repeatedly moving her helm.

   (f) Any means of propulsion may be used to help a person or another vessel in danger.

   (g) To get clear after grounding or colliding with another boat or object, a boat may use force applied by the crew of either boat and any equipment other than a propulsion engine.

   (h) Sailing instructions may, in stated circumstances, permit propulsion using an engine or any other method, provided the boat does not gain a significant advantage in the race.

Note: Interpretations of rule 42 are available at the ISAF website (www.sailing.org) or by mail upon request.

43 COMPETITOR CLOTHING AND EQUIPMENT

43.1 (a) Competitors shall not wear or carry clothing or equipment for the purpose of increasing their weight.

(b) Furthermore, a competitor's clothing and equipment shall not weigh more than 8 kilograms, excluding a hiking or trapeze harness and clothing (including footwear) worn only below the knee. Class rules or sailing instructions may specify a lower weight or a higher weight up to 10 kilograms. Class rules may include footwear and other clothing worn below the knee within that weight. A hiking or trapeze harness shall have positive buoyancy and shall not weigh more than 2 kilograms, except that class rules may specify a higher weight up to 4 kilograms. Weights shall be determined as required by Appendix H.

(c) When an equipment inspector or a measurer in charge of weighing clothing and equipment believes a competitor may have broken rule 43.1(a) or 43.1(b) he shall report the matter in writing to the race committee.

43.2 Rule 43.1(b) does not apply to boats required to be equipped with lifelines.

44 PENALTIES AT THE TIME OF AN INCIDENT

44.1 Taking a Penalty

A boat may take a Two-Turns Penalty when she may have broken a rule of Part 2 while *racing* or a One-Turn Penalty when she may have broken rule 31. Sailing instructions may specify the use of the Scoring Penalty or some other penalty. However,

(a) when a boat may have broken a rule of Part 2 and rule 31 in the same incident she need not take the penalty for breaking rule 31;

(b) if the boat caused injury or serious damage or gained a significant advantage in the race or series by her breach her penalty shall be to retire.

44.2 One-Turn and Two-Turns Penalties

After getting well clear of other boats as soon after the incident as possible, a boat takes a One-Turn or Two-Turns Penalty by promptly making the required number of turns in the same direction, each turn including one tack and one gybe. When a boat takes the penalty at or near the finishing line, she shall sail completely to the course side of the line before *finishing*.

44.3 Scoring Penalty

(a) A boat takes a Scoring Penalty by displaying a yellow flag at the first reasonable opportunity after the incident.

(b) When a boat has taken a Scoring Penalty, she shall keep the yellow flag displayed until *finishing* and call the race committee's attention to it at the finishing line. At that time she shall also inform the race committee of the identity of the other boat involved in the incident. If this is impracticable, she shall do so at the first reasonable opportunity and within the time limit for *protests*.

(c) The race score for a boat that takes a Scoring Penalty shall be the score she would have received without that penalty, made worse by the number of places stated in the sailing instructions. However, she shall not be scored worse than Did Not Finish. When the sailing instructions do not state the number of places, the number shall be the whole number (rounding 0.5 upward) nearest to 20% of the number of boats entered. The scores of other boats shall not be changed; therefore, two boats may receive the same score.

45   HAULING OUT; MAKING FAST; ANCHORING

A boat shall be afloat and off moorings at her preparatory signal. Thereafter, she shall not be hauled out or made fast except to bail out, reef sails or make repairs. She may anchor or the crew may stand on the bottom. She shall recover the anchor before continuing in the race unless she is unable to do so.

46   PERSON IN CHARGE

A boat shall have on board a person in charge designated by the member or organization that entered the boat. See rule 75.

47   LIMITATIONS ON EQUIPMENT AND CREW

47.1 A boat shall use only the equipment on board at her preparatory signal.

47.2 No person on board shall intentionally leave, except when ill or injured, or to help a person or vessel in danger, or to swim. A person leaving the boat by accident or to swim shall be back on board before the boat continues in the race.

48   FOG SIGNALS AND LIGHTS

When safety requires, a boat shall sound fog signals and show lights as required by the *International Regulations for Preventing Collisions at Sea* or applicable government rules.

US SAILING prescribes that the use of additional special-purpose lights such as masthead, spreader and jib-luff lights shall not constitute a breach of this rule.

49   CREW POSITION

49.1 Competitors shall use no device designed to position their bodies outboard, other than hiking straps and stiffeners worn under the thighs.

49.2 When lifelines are required by the class rules or the sailing instructions they shall be taut, and competitors shall not position any part of their torsos outside them, except briefly to perform a necessary task. On boats equipped with upper and lower lifelines of wire, a competitor sitting on the deck facing outboard with his waist inside the lower lifeline may have the upper part of his body outside the upper lifeline.

50   SETTING AND SHEETING SAILS

50.1 Changing Sails

When headsails or spinnakers are being changed, a replacing sail may be fully set and trimmed before the replaced sail is lowered. However, only one mainsail and, except when changing, only one spinnaker shall be carried set at a time.

50.2 Spinnaker Poles; Whisker Poles

Only one spinnaker pole or whisker pole shall be used at a time except when gybing. When in use, it shall be attached to the foremost mast.

50.3 Use of Outriggers

   (a) No sail shall be sheeted over or through an outrigger, except as permitted in rule 50.3(b) or 50.3(c). An outrigger is any fitting or other device so placed that it could exert outward pressure on a sheet or sail at a point from which, with the boat upright, a vertical line would fall outside the hull or deck planking. For the purpose of this rule, bulwarks, rails and rubbing strakes are not part of the hull or deck planking and the following are not outriggers: a bowsprit used to secure the tack of a working sail, a bumkin used to sheet the boom of a working sail, or a boom of a boomed headsail that requires no adjustment when tacking.

   (b) Any sail may be sheeted to or led above a boom that is regularly used for a working sail and is permanently attached to the mast from which the head of the working sail is set.

   (c) A headsail may be sheeted or attached at its clew to a spinnaker pole or whisker pole, provided that a spinnaker is not set.

50.4 Headsails

The difference between a headsail and a spinnaker is that the mid-girth of a headsail, measured from the mid-points of its luff and leech, does not exceed 50% of the length of its foot, and no other intermediate girth exceeds a percentage similarly proportional to its distance from the head of the sail. A sail tacked down behind the foremost mast is not a headsail.

51   MOVABLE BALLAST

All movable ballast, including sails that are not set, shall be properly stowed. Water, dead weight or ballast shall not be moved for the purpose of changing trim or stability. Floorboards, bulkheads, doors, stairs and water tanks shall be left in place and all cabin fixtures kept on board. However, bilge water may be bailed out.

52   MANUAL POWER

A boat's standing rigging, running rigging, spars and movable hull appendages shall be adjusted and operated only by manual power.

53   SKIN FRICTION

A boat shall not eject or release a substance, such as a polymer, or have specially textured surfaces that could improve the character of the flow of water inside the boundary layer.

54   FORESTAYS AND HEADSAIL TACKS

Forestays and headsail tacks, except those of spinnaker staysails when the boat is not close-hauled, shall be attached approximately on a boat's centreline.

55   *FLAGS*

US SAILING prescribes that a boat shall not display flags except for signaling. A boat shall not be penalized for breaking this rule without prior warning and opportunity to make correction.

Part 5 — Protests, Redress, Hearings, Misconduct and Appeals

Section A — Protests; Redress; Rule 69 Action

60 RIGHT TO PROTEST; RIGHT TO REQUEST REDRESS OR RULE 69 ACTION

60.1 A boat may

(a) protest another boat, but not for an alleged breach of a rule of Part 2 unless she was involved in or saw the incident; or

(b) request redress.

60.2 A race committee may

(a) protest a boat, but not as a result of information arising from a request for redress or an invalid *protest*, or from a report from an *interested party* other than the representative of the boat herself;

(b) request redress for a boat; or

(c) report to the protest committee requesting action under rule 69.1(a).

However, when the race committee receives a report required by rule 43.1(c) or 78.3, it shall protest the boat.

60.3 A protest committee may

(a) protest a boat, but not as a result of information arising from a request for redress or an invalid *protest*, or from a report from an *interested party* other than the representative of the boat herself. However, it may protest a boat

(1) if it learns of an incident involving her that may have resulted in injury or serious damage, or

(2) if during the hearing of a valid *protest* it learns that the boat, although not a *party* to the hearing, was involved in the incident and may have broken a *rule*;

(b) call a hearing to consider redress; or

(c) act under rule 69.1(a).

61 PROTEST REQUIREMENTS

61.1 Informing the Protestee

(a) A boat intending to protest shall inform the other boat at the first reasonable opportunity. When her *protest* concerns an incident in the racing area that she is involved in or sees, she shall hail 'Protest' and conspicuously display a red flag at the first reasonable opportunity for each. She shall display the flag until she is no longer *racing*. However,

(1) if the other boat is beyond hailing distance, the protesting boat need not hail but she shall inform the other boat at the first reasonable opportunity;

(2) if the hull length of the protesting boat is less than 6 metres, she need not display a red flag;

(3) if the incident results in damage or injury that is obvious to the boats involved and one of them intends to protest, the requirements of this rule do not apply to her, but she shall attempt to inform the other boat within the time limit of rule 61.3.

(b) A race committee or protest committee intending to protest a boat shall inform her as soon as reasonably possible. However, if the *protest* arises from an incident the committee observes in the racing area, it shall inform the boat after the race within the time limit of rule 61.3.

(c) If the protest committee decides to protest a boat under rule 60.3(a)(2), it shall inform her as soon as reasonably possible, close the current hearing, proceed as required by rules 61.2 and 63, and hear the original and the new *protests* together.

61.2 Protest Contents

A *protest* shall be in writing and identify

(a) the protestor and protestee;

(b) the incident, including where and when it occurred;

(c) any *rule* the protestor believes was broken; and

(d) the name of the protestor's representative.

However, if requirement (b) is met, requirement (a) may be met at any time before the hearing, and requirements (c) and (d) may be met before or during the hearing.

61.3 Protest Time Limit

A *protest* by a boat, or by the race committee or protest committee about an incident the committee observes in the racing area, shall be delivered to the race office within the time limit stated in the sailing instructions. If none is stated, the time limit is two hours after the last boat in the race *finishes*. Other race committee or protest committee *protests* shall be delivered to the race office no later than two hours after the committee receives the relevant information. The protest committee shall extend the time if there is good reason to do so.

61.4 *Fees for Protests and Requests for Redress*
US SAILING prescribes that no fees shall be charged for protests *or requests for redress.*

62 REDRESS

62.1 A request for redress or a protest committee's decision to consider redress shall be based on a claim or possibility that a boat's score in a race or series has, through no fault of her own, been made significantly worse by

(a) an improper action or omission of the race committee, protest committee or organizing authority, but not by a protest committee decision when the boat was a *party* to the hearing;

(b) injury or physical damage because of the action of a boat that was breaking a rule of Part 2 or of a vessel not *racing* that was required to keep clear;

(c) giving help (except to herself or her crew) in compliance with rule 1.1; or

(d) a boat against which a penalty has been imposed under rule 2 or disciplinary action has been taken under rule 69.1(b).

62.2 The request shall be in writing and be delivered to the race office no later than the protest time limit or two hours after the incident, whichever is later. The protest committee shall extend the time if there is good reason to do so. No red flag is required.

Section B — Hearings and Decisions

63 HEARINGS

63.1 Requirement for a Hearing

A boat or competitor shall not be penalized without a protest hearing, except as provided in rules 30.2, 30.3, 67, 69, A5 and P2. A decision on redress shall not be made without a hearing. The protest committee shall hear all *protests* and requests for redress that have been delivered to the race office unless it allows a *protest* or request to be withdrawn.

63.2 Time and Place of the Hearing; Time for Parties to Prepare

All *parties* to the hearing shall be notified of the time and place of the hearing, the *protest* or redress information shall be made available to them, and they shall be allowed reasonable time to prepare for the hearing.

63.3 Right to Be Present

(a) The *parties* to the hearing, or a representative of each, have the right to be present throughout the hearing of all the evidence. When a *protest* claims a breach of a rule of Part 2, 3 or 4, the representatives of boats shall have been on board at the time of the incident, unless there is good reason for the protest committee to rule otherwise. Any witness, other than a member of the protest committee, shall be excluded except when giving evidence.

(b) If a *party* to the hearing of a *protest* or request for redress does not come to the hearing, the protest committee may nevertheless decide the *protest* or request. If the *party* was unavoidably absent, the committee may reopen the hearing.

63.4 Interested Party

A member of a protest committee who is an *interested party* shall not take any further part in the hearing but may appear as a witness. Protest committee members must declare any possible self-interest as soon as they are aware of it. A *party* to the hearing who believes a member of the protest committee is an *interested party* shall object as soon as possible.

63.5 Validity of the Protest or Request for Redress

At the beginning of the hearing the protest committee shall take any evidence it considers necessary to decide whether all requirements for the *protest* or request for redress have been met. If they have been met, the *protest* or request is valid and the hearing shall be continued. If not, the committee shall declare the *protest* or request invalid and close the hearing. If the *protest* has been made under rule 60.3(a)(1), the committee shall also determine whether or not injury or serious damage resulted from the incident in question. If not, the hearing shall be closed.

63.6 Taking Evidence and Finding Facts

The protest committee shall take the evidence of the *parties* to the hearing and of their witnesses and other evidence it considers necessary. A member of the protest committee who saw the incident may give evidence. A *party* to the hearing may question any person who gives evidence. The committee shall then find the facts and base its decision on them.

63.7 Conflict between the Notice of Race and the Sailing Instructions

If there is a conflict between a rule in the notice of race and one in the sailing instructions that must be resolved before the protest committee can decide a *protest* or request for redress, the committee shall apply the rule that it believes will provide the fairest result for all boats affected.

63.8 Protests between Boats in Different Races

A *protest* between boats sailing in different races conducted by different organizing authorities shall be heard by a protest committee acceptable to those authorities.

64 DECISIONS

64.1 Penalties and Exoneration

(a) When the protest committee decides that a boat that is a *party* to a protest hearing has broken a *rule*, it shall disqualify her unless some other penalty applies. A penalty shall be imposed whether or not the applicable *rule* was mentioned in the *protest*.

(b) If a boat has taken an applicable penalty, rule 64.1(a) does not apply to her unless the penalty for a *rule* she broke is a disqualification that is not excludable from her series score.

(c) When as a consequence of breaking a *rule* a boat has compelled another boat to break a *rule*, rule 64.1(a) does not apply to the other boat and she shall be exonerated.

(d) If a boat has broken a *rule* when not *racing*, her penalty shall apply to the race sailed nearest in time to that of the incident.

64.2 Decisions on Redress

When the protest committee decides that a boat is entitled to redress under rule 62, it shall make as fair an arrangement as possible for all boats affected, whether or not they asked for redress. This may be to adjust the scoring (see rule A10 for some examples) or finishing times of boats, to *abandon* the race, to let the results stand or to make some other arrangement. When in doubt about the facts or probable results of any arrangement for the race or series, especially before *abandoning* the race, the protest committee shall take evidence from appropriate sources.

64.3 Decisions on Measurement Protests

(a) When the protest committee finds that deviations in excess of tolerances specified in the class rules were caused by damage or normal wear and do not improve the performance of the boat, it shall not penalize her. However, the boat shall not *race* again until the deviations have been corrected, except when the protest committee decides there is or has been no reasonable opportunity to do so.

(b) When the protest committee is in doubt about the meaning of a measurement rule, it shall refer its questions, together with the relevant facts, to an authority responsible for interpreting the rule. In making its decision, the committee shall be bound by the reply of the authority.

US SAILING prescribes that the authority responsible for interpreting the rules of a handicap or rating system is the organization that issued the handicap or the rating certificate involved.

(c) When a boat disqualified under a measurement rule states in writing that she intends to appeal, she may compete in subsequent races without changes to the boat, but shall be disqualified if she fails to appeal or the appeal is decided against her.

(d) Measurement costs arising from a *protest* involving a measurement rule shall be paid by the unsuccessful *party* unless the protest committee decides otherwise.

65 INFORMING THE PARTIES AND OTHERS

65.1 After making its decision, the protest committee shall promptly inform the *parties* to the hearing of the facts found, the applicable *rules*, the decision, the reasons for it, and any penalties imposed or redress given.

65.2 A *party* to the hearing is entitled to receive the above information in writing, provided she asks for it in writing from the protest committee no later than seven days after being informed of the decision. The committee shall then promptly provide the information, including, when relevant, a diagram of the incident prepared or endorsed by the committee.

65.3 When the protest committee penalizes a boat under a measurement rule, it shall send the above information to the relevant measurement authorities.

66   REOPENING A HEARING

The protest committee may reopen a hearing when it decides that it may have made a significant error, or when significant new evidence becomes available within a reasonable time. It shall reopen a hearing when required by the national authority under rule F6. A *party* to the hearing may ask for a reopening no later than 24 hours after being informed of the decision. When a hearing is reopened, a majority of the members of the protest committee shall, if possible, be members of the original protest committee.

67   RULE 42 AND HEARING REQUIREMENT

When so stated in the sailing instructions, the protest committee may penalize without a hearing a boat that has broken rule 42, provided that a member of the committee or its designated observer has seen the incident, and a disqualification under this rule shall not be excluded from the boat's series score. A boat so penalized shall be informed by notification in the race results.

68   DAMAGES

The question of damages arising from a breach of any *rule* shall be governed by the prescriptions, if any, of the national authority.

US SAILING prescribes that:

(a) **A boat that retires from a race or accepts a penalty does not, by that action alone, admit liability for damages.**

(b) **A protest committee shall find facts and make decisions only in compliance with the rules.**

*No protest committee or US SAILING appeal
authority shall adjudicate any claim for damages.
Such a claim is subject to the jurisdiction of the
courts.*

(c) *A basic purpose of the* rules *is to prevent contact
between boats. By participating in an event governed by the* rules, *a boat agrees that responsibility
for damages arising from any breach of the* rules
*shall be based on fault as determined by appli-
cation of the* rules, *and that she shall not be
governed by the legal doctrine of 'assumption
of risk' for monetary damages resulting from
contact with other boats.*

Section C — Gross Misconduct

69   ALLEGATIONS OF GROSS MISCONDUCT

69.1   Action by a Protest Committee

(a)   When a protest committee, from its own observation
or a report received from any source, believes that a
competitor may have committed a gross breach of
a *rule*, good manners or sportsmanship, or may have
brought the sport into disrepute, it may call a hearing.
The protest committee shall promptly inform the
competitor in writing of the alleged misconduct and
of the time and place of the hearing. If the competitor
provides good reason for being unable to attend the
hearing, the protest committee shall reschedule it.

(b)   A protest committee of at least three members shall
conduct the hearing, following the procedures in rules
63.2, 63.3(a), 63.4 and 63.6. If it decides that the
competitor committed the alleged misconduct it
shall either

(1)   warn the competitor or

(2)   impose a penalty by excluding the competitor and,
when appropriate, disqualifying a boat, from a race
or the remaining races or all races of the series,
or by taking other action within its jurisdiction.
A disqualification under this rule shall not be
excluded from the boat's series score.

(c) The protest committee shall promptly report a penalty, but not a warning, to the national authorities of the venue, of the competitor and of the boat owner. If the protest committee is an international jury appointed by the ISAF under rule 89.2(b), it shall send a copy of the report to the ISAF.

(d) If the competitor does not provide good reason for being unable to attend the hearing and does not come to it, the protest committee may conduct it without the competitor present. If the committee does so and penalizes the competitor, it shall include in the report it makes under rule 69.1(c) the facts found, the decision and the reasons for it.

(e) If the protest committee chooses not to conduct the hearing without the competitor present or if the hearing cannot be scheduled for a time and place when it would be reasonable for the competitor to attend, the protest committee shall collect all available information and, if the allegation seems justified, make a report to the relevant national authorities. If the protest committee is an international jury appointed by the ISAF under rule 89.2(b), it shall send a copy of the report to the ISAF.

(f) When the protest committee has left the event and a report alleging misconduct is received, the race committee or organizing authority may appoint a new protest committee to proceed under this rule.

69.2 Action by a National Authority or Initial Action by the ISAF

(a) When a national authority or the ISAF receives a report alleging a gross breach of a *rule*, good manners or sportsmanship, a report alleging conduct that has brought the sport into disrepute, or a report required by rule 69.1(c) or 69.1(e), it may conduct an investigation and, when appropriate, shall conduct a hearing. It may then take any disciplinary action within its jurisdiction it considers appropriate against the competitor or boat, or other person involved, including suspending eligibility, permanently or for a specified period of time, to compete in any event held within its jurisdiction, and suspending ISAF eligibility under ISAF Regulation 19.

(b) The national authority of a competitor shall also suspend the ISAF eligibility of the competitor as required in ISAF Regulation 19.

(c) The national authority shall promptly report a suspension of eligibility under rule 69.2(a) to the ISAF, and to the national authorities of the person or the owner of the boat suspended if they are not members of the suspending national authority.

69.3 Subsequent Action by the ISAF

Upon receipt of a report required by rule 69.2(c) or ISAF Regulation 19, or following its own action under rule 69.2(a), the ISAF shall inform all national authorities, which may also suspend eligibility for events held within their jurisdiction. The ISAF Executive Committee shall suspend the competitor's ISAF eligibility as required in ISAF Regulation 19 if the competitor's national authority does not do so.

Section D — Appeals

70 APPEALS AND REQUESTS TO A NATIONAL AUTHORITY

70.1 Provided that the right of appeal has not been denied under rule 70.5, a *party* to a hearing may appeal a protest committee's decision or its procedures, but not the facts found.

70.2 A protest committee may request confirmation or correction of its decision.

70.3 An appeal under rule 70.1 or a request by a protest committee under rule 70.2 shall be sent to the national authority with which the organizing authority is associated under rule 89.1. However, if boats will pass through the waters of more than one national authority while *racing*, the sailing instructions shall identify the national authority to which appeals or requests may be sent.

70.4 A club or other organization affiliated to a national authority may request an interpretation of the *rules*, provided that no *protest* or request for redress that may be appealed is involved. The interpretation shall not be used for changing a previous protest committee decision.

70.5 There shall be no appeal from the decisions of an international jury constituted in compliance with Appendix N. Furthermore, if the notice of race and the sailing instructions so state, the right of appeal may be denied provided that

  (a) it is essential to determine promptly the result of a race that will qualify a boat to compete in a later stage of an event or a subsequent event (a national authority may prescribe that its approval is required for such a procedure);

  US SAILING prescribes that its approval is required.

  See www.ussailing.org/rules/noappeal for more information or to obtain approval.

  (b) a national authority so approves for a particular event open only to entrants under its own jurisdiction; or

  (c) a national authority after consultation with the ISAF so approves for a particular event, provided the protest committee is constituted as required by Appendix N, except that only two members of the protest committee need be International Judges.

70.6 Appeals and requests shall conform to Appendix F.

71 NATIONAL AUTHORITY DECISIONS

71.1 No *interested party* or member of the protest committee shall take any part in the discussion or decision on an appeal or a request for confirmation or correction.

71.2 The national authority may uphold, change or reverse the protest committee's decision; declare the *protest* or request for redress invalid; or return the *protest* or request for the hearing to be reopened, or for a new hearing and decision by the same or a different protest committee.

71.3 When from the facts found by the protest committee the national authority decides that a boat that was a *party* to a protest hearing broke a *rule*, it shall penalize her, whether or not that boat or that *rule* was mentioned in the protest committee's decision.

71.4 The decision of the national authority shall be final. The national authority shall send its decision in writing to all *parties* to the hearing and the protest committee, who shall be bound by the decision.

Part 6 — Entry and Qualification

75   ENTERING A RACE

75.1   To enter a race, a boat shall comply with the requirements of the organizing authority of the race. She shall be entered by
   (a)   a member of a club or other organization affiliated to an ISAF member national authority,
   (b)   such a club or organization, or
   (c)   a member of an ISAF member national authority.

75.2   Competitors shall comply with ISAF Regulation 19, Eligibility Code.

76   EXCLUSION OF BOATS OR COMPETITORS

76.1   The organizing authority or the race committee may reject or cancel the entry of a boat or exclude a competitor, subject to rule 76.2, provided it does so before the start of the first race and states the reason for doing so. However, the organizing authority or the race committee shall not reject or cancel the entry of a boat or exclude a competitor because of advertising, provided the boat or competitor complies with ISAF Regulation 20, Advertising Code.

US SAILING prescribes that an organizing authority or race committee shall not reject or cancel the entry of a boat or exclude a competitor eligible under the notice of race and sailing instructions for an arbitrary or capricious reason or for reason of race, color, religion, national origin, gender, sexual orientation, or age.

76.2   At world and continental championships no entry within stated quotas shall be rejected or cancelled without first obtaining the approval of the relevant international class association (or the Offshore Racing Council) or the ISAF.

76.3   *US SAILING prescribes that a boat whose entry is rejected or cancelled or a competitor who is excluded from a race or series shall be, upon written request, entitled to a hearing conducted by the protest committee under rules 63.2, 63.3, 63.4 and 63.6.*

77   IDENTIFICATION ON SAILS

A boat shall comply with the requirements of Appendix G governing class insignia, national letters and numbers on sails.

78   COMPLIANCE WITH CLASS RULES; CERTIFICATES

78.1   A boat's owner and any other person in charge shall ensure that the boat is maintained to comply with her class rules and that her measurement or rating certificate, if any, remains valid.

78.2   When a *rule* requires a certificate to be produced before a boat *races*, and it is not produced, the boat may *race* provided that the race committee receives a statement signed by the person in charge that a valid certificate exists and that it will be given to the race committee before the end of the event. If the certificate is not received in time, the boat shall be disqualified from all races of the event.

78.3   When an equipment inspector or a measurer for an event decides that a boat or personal equipment does not comply with the class rules, he shall report the matter in writing to the race committee.

79   CLASSIFICATION

If the notice of race or class rules state that some or all competitors must satisfy classification requirements, the classification shall be carried out as described in ISAF Regulation 22, Sailor Classification Code.

80   ADVERTISING

A boat and her crew shall comply with ISAF Regulation 20, Advertising Code.

81   RESCHEDULED RACES

When a race has been rescheduled, all boats entered in the original race shall be notified. New entries that meet the entry requirements of the original race may be accepted at the discretion of the race committee.

82   *INDEMNIFICATION OR HOLD HARMLESS AGREEMENTS*

US SAILING prescribes that the organizing authority shall not require a competitor to assume any liabilities of the organizing authority, race committee, protest committee, host club, sponsors, or any other organization or official involved with the event. (This is commonly referred to as an 'indemnification' or 'hold harmless' agreement.)

See www.ussailing.org/rules/indemnification for more information.

Part 7 — Race Organization

85 GOVERNING RULES

The organizing authority, race committee and protest committee shall be governed by the *rules* in the conduct and judging of races.

86 CHANGES TO THE RACING RULES

86.1 A racing rule shall not be changed unless permitted in the rule itself or as follows:

(a) Prescriptions of a national authority may change a racing rule, but not the Definitions; a rule in the Introduction; Sportsmanship and the Rules; Part 1, 2 or 7; rule 42, 43, 69, 70, 71, 75, 76.2, 79 or 80; a rule of an appendix that changes one of these rules; Appendix H or N; or ISAF Regulation 19, 20, 21 or 22.

(b) Sailing instructions may change a racing rule, but not rule 76.1, Appendix F, or a rule listed in rule 86.1(a). However, the sailing instructions may change to 'two' or 'four' the number of hull lengths determining the *zone* around *marks*, provided that the number is the same for all *marks* and all boats using those *marks*. If the sailing instructions change a rule or that definition, they shall refer specifically to the rule or definition and state the change.

(c) Class rules may change only racing rules 42, 49, 50, 51, 52, 53 and 54. Such changes shall refer specifically to the rule and state the change.

Note: The second sentence of this rule takes effect on 1 January 2011.

86.2 In exception to rule 86.1, the ISAF may in limited circumstances (see ISAF Regulation 31.1.3) authorize changes to the racing rules for a specific international event. The authorization shall be stated in a letter of approval to the event organizing authority and in the notice of race and sailing instructions, and the letter shall be posted on the event's official notice board.

86.3 If a national authority so prescribes, the restrictions in rule 86.1 do not apply if rules are changed to develop or test proposed rules. The national authority may prescribe that its approval is required for such changes.

*US SAILING prescribes that proposed rules may be
tested, but only in local races. However, proposed
rules may also be tested at other events if, for each
event, the organizing authority first obtains written
permission from US SAILING and the proposed
rules are included in the notice of race and sailing
instructions.*

87 CHANGES TO CLASS RULES

The sailing instructions may change a class rule only when
the class rules permit the change, or when written permission of the class association for the change is displayed
on the official notice board.

88 NATIONAL PRESCRIPTIONS

88.1 The prescriptions that apply to an event are the prescriptions of the national authority with which the organizing
authority is associated under rule 89.1. However, if boats
will pass through the waters of more than one national
authority while *racing*, the sailing instructions shall identify
any other prescriptions that will apply and when they will
apply.

88.2 The sailing instructions may change a prescription.
However, a national authority may restrict changes to its
prescriptions with a prescription to this rule, provided the
ISAF approves its application to do so. The restricted prescriptions shall not be changed by the sailing instructions.

*US SAILING prescribes that sailing instructions shall
not change or delete rules 61.4 or 76.3, Appendix F,
or its prescriptions to rules 40, 68, 70.5(a) or 76.1.
However, for an international event the prescription
to rule 40 may be deleted.*

89 ORGANIZING AUTHORITY; NOTICE OF RACE; APPOINTMENT OF RACE OFFICIALS

89.1 Organizing Authority

Races shall be organized by an organizing authority, which
shall be

(a) the ISAF;

(b) a member national authority of the ISAF;

(c) a club or other organization affiliated to a national
authority;

(d) a class association, either with the approval of a national authority or in conjunction with an affiliated club;

(e) an unaffiliated body in conjunction with an affiliated club where the body is owned and controlled by the club. The national authority of the club may prescribe that its approval is required for such an event; or

(f) if approved by the ISAF and the national authority of the club, an unaffiliated body in conjunction with an affiliated club where the body is not owned and controlled by the club.

89.2 Notice of Race; Appointment of Race Officials

(a) The organizing authority shall publish a notice of race that conforms to rule J1. The notice of race may be changed provided adequate notice is given.

(b) The organizing authority shall appoint a race committee and, when appropriate, appoint a protest committee and umpires. However, the race committee, an international jury and umpires may be appointed by the ISAF as provided in the ISAF regulations.

90 RACE COMMITTEE; SAILING INSTRUCTIONS; SCORING

90.1 Race Committee

The race committee shall conduct races as directed by the organizing authority and as required by the *rules*.

90.2 Sailing Instructions

(a) The race committee shall publish written sailing instructions that conform to rule J2.

(b) When appropriate, for an event where entries from other countries are expected, the sailing instructions shall include, in English, the applicable national prescriptions.

(c) Changes to the sailing instructions shall be in writing and posted on the official notice board before the time stated in the sailing instructions or, on the water, communicated to each boat before her warning signal. Oral changes may be given only on the water, and only if the procedure is stated in the sailing instructions.

90.3 Scoring

(a) The race committee shall score a race or series as provided in Appendix A using the Low Point System, unless the sailing instructions specify the Bonus Point System or some other system. A race shall be scored if it is not *abandoned* and if one boat sails the course in compliance with rule 28.1 and *finishes* within the time limit, if any, even if she retires after *finishing* or is disqualified.

(b) When a scoring system provides for excluding one or more race scores from a boat's series score, the score for disqualification under rule 2; rule 30.3's last sentence; rule 42 if rule 67, P2.2 or P2.3 applies; or rule 69.1(b)(2) shall not be excluded. The next-worse score shall be excluded instead.

91   PROTEST COMMITTEE

A protest committee shall be

(a) a committee appointed by the organizing authority or race committee, or

(b) an international jury appointed by the organizing authority or as prescribed in the ISAF regulations and meeting the requirements of Appendix N. A national authority may prescribe that its approval is required for the appointment of international juries for races within its jurisdiction, except ISAF events or when international juries are appointed by the ISAF under rule 89.2(b).

Appendix A — Scoring

See rule 90.3.

A1 NUMBER OF RACES

The number of races scheduled and the number required to be completed to constitute a series shall be stated in the sailing instructions.

A2 SERIES SCORES

Each boat's series score shall be the total of her race scores excluding her worst score. (The sailing instructions may make a different arrangement by providing, for example, that no score will be excluded, that two or more scores will be excluded, or that a specified number of scores will be excluded if a specified number of races are completed. A race is completed if scored; see rule 90.3(a).) If a boat has two or more equal worst scores, the score(s) for the race(s) sailed earliest in the series shall be excluded. The boat with the lowest series score wins and others shall be ranked accordingly.

A3 STARTING TIMES AND FINISHING PLACES

The time of a boat's starting signal shall be her starting time, and the order in which boats *finish* a race shall determine their finishing places. However, when a handicap or rating system is used a boat's corrected time shall determine her finishing place.

A4 LOW POINT AND BONUS POINT SYSTEMS

Most series are scored using either the Low Point System or the Bonus Point System. The Low Point System uses a boat's finishing place as her race score. The Bonus Point System benefits the first six finishers because of the greater difficulty in advancing from fourth place to third, for example, than from fourteenth place to thirteenth. The Low Point System will apply unless the sailing instructions specify another system; see rule 90.3(a). If the Bonus Point System is chosen it can be made to apply by stating in the sailing instructions that 'The Bonus Point System of Appendix A will apply.'

A4.1 Each boat *starting* and *finishing* and not thereafter retiring, being penalized or given redress shall be scored points as follows:

Finishing place	Low Point System	Bonus Point System
First	1	0
Second	2	3
Third	3	5.7
Fourth	4	8
Fifth	5	10
Sixth	6	11.7
Seventh	7	13
Each place thereafter	Add 1 point	Add 1 point

A4.2 A boat that did not *start*, did not *finish*, retired after *finishing* or was disqualified shall be scored points for the finishing place one more than the number of boats entered in the series. A boat that is penalized under rule 30.2 or that takes a penalty under rule 44.3(a) shall be scored points as provided in rule 44.3(c).

A5 **SCORES DETERMINED BY THE RACE COMMITTEE**

A boat that did not *start*, comply with rule 30.2 or 30.3, or *finish*, or that takes a penalty under rule 44.3(a) or retires after *finishing*, shall be scored accordingly by the race committee without a hearing. Only the protest committee may take other scoring actions that worsen a boat's score.

A6 **CHANGES IN PLACES AND SCORES OF OTHER BOATS**

A6.1 If a boat is disqualified from a race or retires after *finishing*, each boat with a worse finishing place shall be moved up one place.

A6.2 If the protest committee decides to give redress by adjusting a boat's score, the scores of other boats shall not be changed unless the protest committee decides otherwise.

A7 **RACE TIES**

If boats are tied at the finishing line or if a handicap or rating system is used and boats have equal corrected times, the points for the place for which the boats have tied and for the place(s) immediately below shall be added together and divided equally. Boats tied for a race prize shall share it or be given equal prizes.

A8   SERIES TIES

A8.1 If there is a series-score tie between two or more boats, each boat's race scores shall be listed in order of best to worst, and at the first point(s) where there is a difference the tie shall be broken in favour of the boat(s) with the best score(s). No excluded scores shall be used.

A8.2 If a tie remains between two or more boats, they shall be ranked in order of their scores in the last race. Any remaining ties shall be broken by using the tied boats' scores in the next-to-last race and so on until all ties are broken. These scores shall be used even if some of them are excluded scores.

A9   RACE SCORES IN A SERIES LONGER THAN A REGATTA

For a series that is held over a period of time longer than a regatta, a boat that came to the starting area but did not *start*, did not *finish*, retired after *finishing* or was disqualified shall be scored points for the finishing place one more than the number of boats that came to the starting area. A boat that did not come to the starting area shall be scored points for the finishing place one more than the number of boats entered in the series.

A10 GUIDANCE ON REDRESS

If the protest committee decides to give redress by adjusting a boat's score for a race, it is advised to consider scoring her

(a) points equal to the average, to the nearest tenth of a point (0.05 to be rounded upward), of her points in all the races in the series except the race in question;

(b) points equal to the average, to the nearest tenth of a point (0.05 to be rounded upward), of her points in all the races before the race in question; or

(c) points based on the position of the boat in the race at the time of the incident that justified redress.

A11 SCORING ABBREVIATIONS

These scoring abbreviations shall be used for recording the circumstances described:

DNC Did not *start*; did not come to the starting area

DNS Did not *start* (other than DNC and OCS)

OCS Did not *start*; on the course side of the starting line at her starting signal and failed to *start*, or broke rule 30.1

ZFP 20% penalty under rule 30.2

BFD Disqualification under rule 30.3

SCP Took a Scoring Penalty under rule 44.3(a)

DNF Did not *finish*

RAF Retired after *finishing*

DSQ Disqualification

DNE Disqualification (other than DGM) not excludable under rule 90.3(b)

DGM Disqualification for gross misconduct not excludable under rule 90.3(b)

RDG Redress given

US SAILING Note on Scoring a Long Series: The scoring systems in Appendix A may be inappropriate for a long series, such as a club's season championship held over several weeks or months, in which some boats do not compete in all of the races and in which more boats compete in some races than in others. See 'Scoring a Long Series' at www.ussailing.org/rules/longseries for an explanation of the scoring problems that occur in such series, alternative scoring systems, and language for sailing instructions to implement them.

Appendix B — Windsurfing Competition Rules

Windsurfing competition shall be sailed under The Racing Rules of Sailing *as changed by this appendix. The term 'boat' elsewhere in the racing rules means 'board' or 'boat' as appropriate. A windsurfing event can include one or more of the following disciplines or their formats:*

Discipline	Formats
Racing	*Course racing; slalom; marathon*
Expression	*Wave performance; freestyle*
Speed	

In expression competition a board's performance is judged on skill and variety rather than speed and is organized using elimination series. Either wave performance or freestyle competition is organized, depending on the wave conditions at the venue. In speed competition, a 'round' consists of one or more speed runs in which the boards take turns sailing the course at intervals. In the racing discipline a marathon race is a race scheduled to last more than one hour.

In racing or expression competition, 'heat' means one elimination contest, a 'round' consists of one or more heats, and an elimination series consists of one or more rounds.

B1 DEFINITIONS

B1.1 The following additional definitions apply:

About to Round or Pass A board is *about to round or pass* a *mark* when her *proper course* is to begin to manoeuvre to round or pass it.

Beach Start When the starting line is on the beach, or so close to the beach that the competitor must stand in the water to *start*, the start is a *beach start*.

Capsized A board is *capsized* when her sail or the competitor is in the water.

B1.2 The following definitions apply only to expression competition:

Coming In and **Going Out** A board sailing in the same direction as the incoming surf is *coming in*. A board sailing in the direction opposite to the incoming surf is *going out*.

Jumping A board is *jumping* when she takes off at the top of a wave while *going out*.

Overtaking A board is *overtaking* from the moment she gains an *overlap* from *clear astern* until the moment she is *clear ahead* of the *overtaken* board.

Possession The first board sailing shoreward immediately in front of a wave has *possession* of that wave. However, when it is impossible to determine which board is first the *windward* board has *possession*.

Recovering A board is *recovering* from the time her sail or, when water-starting, the competitor is out of the water until she has steerage way.

Surfing A board is *surfing* when she is on or immediately in front of a wave while *coming in*.

Transition A board changing *tacks*, or taking off while *coming in*, or one that is not *surfing*, *jumping*, *capsized* or *recovering* is in *transition*.

B2 RULES FOR ALL COMPETITION
Rule B2 applies to all competition.

B2.1 Changes to the Rules of Part 4
(a) Rule 42 is changed to 'A board shall be propelled only by the action of the wind on the sail, by the action of the water on the hull and by the unassisted actions of the competitor.'

(b) Add to rule 43.1(a): 'However, a competitor may wear a drinking container that shall have a capacity of at least one litre and weigh no more than 1.5 kilograms when full.'

(c) Rule 44.2 is changed so that two turns are replaced by one 360° turn with no requirement for tacks or gybes.

(d) Add to rule 47.1: 'except as stated in rule 41.2'. (See rule B4.4.)

B2.2 Entry and Qualification
Add to rule 78.1: 'When so prescribed by the ISAF, a numbered and dated device on a board and her centreboard, fin and rig shall serve as her measurement certificate.'

B2.3 Event Organization
(a) The last sentence of rule 90.2(c) is deleted.

(b) Add new rule 90.2(d): 'Oral instructions may be given only if the procedure is stated in the sailing instructions.'

B2.4 Identification on Sails

(a) Add to rule G1.1(a): 'The insignia shall not refer to anything other than the manufacturer or class and shall not consist of more than two letters and three numbers or an abstract design.'

(b) Rules G1.3(a), G1.3(c), G1.3(d) and G1.3(e) are changed to

The class insignia shall be displayed once on each side of the sail in the area above a line projected at right angles from a point on the luff of the sail one-third of the distance from the head to the wishbone. The national letters and sail numbers shall be in the central third of that part of the sail above the wishbone, clearly separated from any advertising. They shall be black and applied back to back on an opaque white background. The background shall extend a minimum of 30 mm beyond the characters. Between the national letters and sail number a '–' and normal spacing shall be applied.

B2.5 Touching a Mark

Rule 31 is changed to 'A board may touch a *mark* but shall not hold on to it.'

B2.6 Deleted Rules

Rules 17, 18.3, 43.2, 44.3, 45, 47.2, 48, 49, 50, 51, 52, 54, 61.1(a)(2), 67, J2.2(28) and J2.2(33) are deleted.

B3 RULES FOR RACING COMPETITION

Rule B3 applies to racing competition. Rule B2 also applies.

B3.1 Changes to the Rules of Part 2, Section C

(a) The first sentence of rule 18.1 is changed to 'Rule 18 applies between boards when they are required to leave a *mark* on the same side and at least one of them is *about to round or pass* it.'

(b) Rule 18.2(b) is changed to

If boards are *overlapped* when the first of them is *about to round or pass* the *mark*, the outside board at that moment shall thereafter give the inside board *mark-room*. If a board is *clear ahead* when she is *about to round or pass* the *mark*, the board *clear astern* at that moment shall thereafter give her *mark-room*.

(c) Rule 18.2(c) is changed to

When a board is required to give *mark-room* by rule 18.2(b), she shall continue to do so even if later an *overlap* is broken or a new *overlap* begins. However, if either board passes head to wind rule 18.2(b) ceases to apply.

(d) Rule 18.4 is changed to

When an inside *overlapped* right-of-way board must gybe or bear away at a *mark* to sail her *proper course*, until she gybes or bears away she shall sail no farther from the *mark* than needed to sail that course. Rule 18.4 does not apply at a gate *mark*.

B3.2 Changes to Other Rules of Part 2

(a) In the preamble of Part 2, 'rule 23.1' is changed to 'rules 23.1 and 23.3'.

(b) Add new rule 16.3:

In slalom racing, a right-of-way board shall not change course during the last 30 seconds before her starting signal if as a result the other board would have to take immediate action to avoid contact.

(c) Rule 22 becomes rule 22.1 and its last sentence is deleted. Add new rule 22.2: 'A *capsized* board shall not take an action that hinders another board.'

(d) Rule 23.1 is changed to 'If reasonably possible, a board not *racing* shall not interfere with a board that is *racing*. After *finishing*, a board shall immediately clear the finishing line and *marks* and avoid boards still *racing*.'

(e) Add new rule 23.3: 'A board shall not sail in the course area defined in the sailing instructions when races are taking place except in her own race.'

(f) Add new rule 24:

24 SAIL OUT OF THE WATER WHEN STARTING

When approaching the starting line to *start*, a board shall have her sail out of the water and in a normal position, except when accidentally *capsized*.

B3.3 Starting Races

The sailing instructions shall specify one of these starting systems.

(a) SYSTEM 1

See rule 26, Starting Races.

(b) SYSTEM 2

Races shall be started by using the following signals.
Times shall be taken from the visual signals; the
absence of a sound signal shall be disregarded.

Signal	Flag and sound	Minutes before starting signal
Attention	Class flag or heat number	3
Warning	Red flag; attention signal removed; 1 sound	2
Preparatory	Yellow flag; red flag removed; 1 sound	1
	Yellow flag removed	1/2
Starting	Green flag; 1 sound	0

(c) SYSTEM 3 (FOR BEACH STARTS)

(1) Before her start each board in a heat or class shall
draw a number for her station on the starting line.
The stations shall be numbered so that station 1
is the most windward one.

(2) After boards have been called to take their positions, the race committee shall make the preparatory signal by displaying a red flag with one
sound. The starting signal shall be made, at any
time after the preparatory signal, by removing
the red flag with one sound.

(3) After the starting signal each board shall take the
shortest route from her starting station to her windsurfing position in the water (with both of the
competitor's feet on the board).

B3.4 Other Rules for the Conduct of a Race

Add new rule 29.3:

29.3 Recall for a Slalom Race

(a) When at a board's starting signal for a slalom race
or heat any part of her hull, crew or equipment is
on the course side of the starting line, the race
committee shall signal a general recall.

(b) If the race committee acts under rule 29.3(a) and
the board is identified, she shall be disqualified
without a hearing, even if the race or heat is
abandoned. The race committee shall hail or
display her sail number, and she shall leave

the course area immediately. If the race or heat is restarted or resailed, she shall not sail in it.

(c) If a slalom race or heat was completed but was later *abandoned* by the protest committee and if the race or heat is resailed, a board disqualified under rule 29.3(b) may sail in it.

B4 RULES FOR EXPRESSION COMPETITION

B4.1 Right-of-Way Rules

These rules replace all rules of Part 2.

(a) COMING IN AND GOING OUT

A board *coming in* shall *keep clear* of a board *going out*. When two boards are *going out* or *coming in* while on the same wave, or when neither is *going out* or *coming in*, a board on *port tack* shall *keep clear* of one on *starboard tack*.

(b) BOARDS ON THE SAME WAVE, COMING IN

When two or more boards are on a wave *coming in*, a board that does not have *possession* shall *keep clear*.

(c) CLEAR ASTERN, CLEAR AHEAD AND OVERTAKING

A board *clear astern* and not on a wave shall *keep clear* of a board *clear ahead*. An *overtaking* board that is not on a wave shall *keep clear*.

(d) TRANSITION

A board in *transition* shall *keep clear* of one that is not. When two boards are in *transition* at the same time, the one on the other's port side or the one astern shall *keep clear*.

B4.2 Starting and Ending Heats

Heats shall be started and ended by using the following signals:

(a) STARTING A HEAT

Each flag shall be removed when the next flag is displayed.

Signal	Flag and sound	Minutes before starting signal
Attention	Heat number	3
Warning	Red flag; 1 sound	2
Preparatory	Yellow flag; 1 sound	1
Starting	Green flag; 1 sound	0

(b) ENDING A HEAT

Signal	Flag and sound	Minutes before ending signal
End warning	Green flag removed; 1 sound	1
Ending	Red flag; 1 sound	0

B4.3 Registration of Sails; Course Area; Heat Duration

(a) Boards shall register with the race committee the colours and other particulars of their sails, or their identification according to another method stated in the sailing instructions, no later than the starting signal for the heat two heats before their own.

(b) The course area shall be defined in the sailing instructions and posted on the official notice board no later than 10 minutes before the starting signal for the first heat. A board shall be scored only while sailing in the course area.

(c) Any change in heat duration shall be announced by the race committee no later than 15 minutes before the starting signal for the first heat in the next round.

B4.4 Outside Help

Rule 41 becomes rule 41.1. Add new rule 41.2:

An assistant may provide replacement equipment to a board but shall keep clear of other boards competing. A board whose assistant fails to keep clear shall be penalized. The penalty shall be at the discretion of the protest committee.

B5 ELIMINATION SERIES

Rule B5 applies when an elimination series is organized in which boards compete in heats.

B5.1 Elimination Series Procedure

(a) Competition shall take the form of one or more elimination series. Each of them shall consist of either a maximum of four rounds in a single elimination series where only a number of the best scorers advance, or a maximum of ten rounds in a double elimination series where boards have more than one opportunity to advance.

(b) Boards shall sail one against another in pairs, or in groups determined by the elimination ladder. The

selected form of competition shall not be changed
while a round remains uncompleted.

B5.2 Seeding and Ranking Lists

(a) When a seeding or ranking list is used to establish
the heats of the first round, places 1–8 (four heats) or
1–16 (eight heats) shall be distributed evenly among
the heats.

(b) For a subsequent elimination series, if any, boards shall
be reassigned to new heats according to the ranking
in the previous elimination series.

(c) The organizing authority's seeding decisions are final
and are not grounds for a request for redress.

B5.3 Heat Schedule

The schedule of heats shall be posted on the official notice
board no later than 30 minutes before the starting signal
for the first heat.

B5.4 Advancement and Byes

(a) In racing and expression competition, the boards
in each heat to advance to the next round shall be
announced by the race committee no later than
10 minutes before the starting signal for the first
heat. The number advancing may be changed by the
protest committee as a result of a redress decision.

(b) In expression competition, any first-round byes shall
be assigned to the highest-seeded boards.

(c) In wave performance competition, only the winner
of each heat shall advance to the next round.
In freestyle competition, boards shall advance to the
next round as follows: from an eight-board heat, the
best four advance, and the winner will sail against
the fourth and the second against the third; from
a four-board heat, the best two advance and will
sail against each other.

B5.5 Finals

(a) The final shall consist of a maximum of three races.
The race committee shall announce the number of
races to be sailed in the final no later than five minutes
before the warning signal for the first final race.

  (b) A runners-up final may be sailed after the final. All
       boards in the semifinal heats that failed to qualify for
       the final may compete in it.

B6   RULES FOR SPEED COMPETITION

B6.1 General Rules

All rules of Part 2 are replaced by relevant parts of this rule.

  (a) BEACH AND WATER STARTING

       A board shall not *beach start* or water start on the
       course or in the starting area, except to sail off the
       course to avoid boards that are *starting* or *racing*.

  (b) LEAVING THE COURSE AREA

       A board leaving the course area shall *keep clear* of
       boards *racing*.

  (c) COURSE CONTROL

       When the race committee points an orange flag at a
       board, she shall immediately leave the course area.

  (d) RETURNING TO THE STARTING AREA

       A board returning to the starting area shall keep clear
       of the course.

  (e) RUN; ROUND

       The maximum number of runs to be made by each
       board in a round shall be announced by the race com-
       mittee no later than 15 minutes before the starting sig-
       nal for the first round.

  (f) DURATION OF A ROUND

       The duration of a round shall be announced by the
       race committee no later than 15 minutes before the
       starting signal for the next round.

  (g) CONDITIONS FOR ESTABLISHING A RECORD

       The minimum distance for a world record is 500
       metres. Other records may be established over short-
       er distances. The course shall be defined by posts and
       transits ashore or by buoys afloat. Transits shall not
       converge.

B6.2 Starting System for Speed Competition

Rounds shall be started and ended by using the following
signals. Each flag shall be removed when the next flag is
displayed.

(a) STARTING A ROUND

Signal	Flag	Meaning
Stand-by	Red flag	Course closed
Course closed	AP and red flag	Course closed; will open shortly
Preparatory	Yellow flag	Course will open in 5 minutes
Starting	Green flag	Course is open

(b) ENDING A ROUND

Signal	Flag	Meaning
End warning	Green and yellow flag	Course will be closed in 5 minutes
Extension	Green flag and L	Current round extended by 15 minutes
Round ended	Red flag and L	A new round will be started shortly

B6.3 Penalties

(a) If a board fails to comply with a warning by the race committee, she may be cautioned and her sail number shall be posted on a notice board near the finishing line.

(b) If a board is cautioned a second time during the same round, she shall be suspended by the race committee from the remainder of the round and her sail number shall be posted on the official notice board.

(c) A board observed in the course area while suspended shall be excluded from the competition without a hearing and none of her previous times or results shall be valid.

(d) Any breach of the verification rules may result in a suspension from the competition for any period.

B6.4 Verification

    (a)   An observer appointed by the World Sailing Speed Record Council (WSSRC) shall be present and verify run times and speeds at world record attempts. The race committee shall verify run times and speeds at other record attempts.

    (b)   A competitor shall not enter the timing control area or discuss any timing matter directly with the timing organization. Any timing question shall be directed to the race committee.

B7   PROTESTS, REDRESS, HEARINGS AND APPEALS

B7.1 The first three sentences of rule 61.1(a) are replaced by

A board intending to protest shall inform the other board at the first reasonable opportunity. When her *protest* concerns an incident in the racing area that she is involved in or sees, she shall hail 'Protest'. She shall inform the race committee of her intention to protest immediately after she *finishes* or retires.

B7.2 In an elimination series, *protests* and requests for redress shall be made orally immediately following the heat in which the incident occurred. The protest committee may take evidence in any way it considers appropriate and may communicate its decision orally.

B7.3 Add new rule 62.1(e): 'a board that failed to *keep clear* and caused *capsize* of the other board.'

B7.4 Add new rule 70.7: 'Appeals are not permitted in disciplines with elimination series.'

B8   SCORING

B8.1 Overall Scores

    If an event includes more than one discipline or format the sailing instructions shall state how the overall score is to be calculated.

B8.2 Series Scores

    Rule A2 is changed to

        Each board's series score shall be the total of her race, elimination series or speed round scores with the number of her worst scores excluded as follows:

Course races	Speed rounds	Slalom and expression elimination series	Number excluded
1–4	1–3	1–2	0
5–11	4–6	3–4	1
12 or more	7–10	5–7	2
	11–15	8 or more	3
	16 or more		4

If a board has two or more equal worst scores, the score(s) for the race(s) sailed earliest in the series shall be excluded. The board with the lowest series score wins and others shall be ranked accordingly. Rules B8.5, B8.6 and B8.7 contain exceptions to this rule.

B8.3 Scoring Systems

Add to the end of the first sentence of rule A4.2: 'or, in an elimination series, the number of boards in that heat'.

B8.4 Uncompleted Heat

When a heat cannot be completed, the points for the unscored places shall be added together and divided by the number of places in that heat. The resulting number of points, to the nearest tenth of a point (0.05 to be rounded upward), shall be given to each board entered in the heat.

B8.5 Scoring a Final Series in Slalom Racing

(a) If three final races are completed, a board's series score in the final shall be the total of her race scores excluding her worst score. Otherwise her series score shall be the total of her race scores.

(b) A board that did not *start*, did not *finish*, retired after *finishing* or was disqualified from a final race shall be scored points equal to the total number of boards entered in the final.

B8.6 Expression Competition Scoring

(a) Expression competition shall be scored by a panel of three judges. However, the panel may have a greater odd number of members, and there may be two such panels. Each judge shall give points for each manoeuvre based on the scale stated in the sailing instructions.

(b) The criteria of scoring shall be decided by the race committee and announced on the official notice board no later than 30 minutes before the starting signal for the first heat.

(c) A board's heat standing shall be determined by adding together the points given by each judge. The board with the highest score wins and others shall be ranked accordingly.

(d) Both semifinal heats shall have been sailed for an elimination series to be valid.

(e) Except for members of the race committee responsible for scoring the event, only competitors in the heat shall be allowed to see judges' score sheets for the heat. Each score sheet shall bear the full name of the judge.

(f) Scoring decisions of the judges shall not be grounds for a request for redress by a board.

B8.7 Speed Competition

The speeds of a board's fastest two runs in a round shall be averaged to determine her standing in that round. The board with the highest average wins and others shall be ranked accordingly.

B8.8 Series Ties

(a) RACING AND SPEED COMPETITION

Rule A8 is changed as follows for racing and speed competition:

(1) Add new rule A8.1: 'If there is a series-score tie between two or more boards, it shall be broken in favour of the board(s) with the best single excluded race score(s).'

(2) Rule A8.1 becomes rule A8.2. Its beginning 'If there is a series-score tie' is changed to 'If a tie remains' and its last sentence is changed to 'These scores shall be used even if some of them are excluded scores.'

(3) Rule A8.2 becomes rule A8.3 and its beginning 'If a tie remains' is changed to 'If a tie still remains'.

(b) EXPRESSION COMPETITION

Rule A8 is changed as follows for expression competition:

(1) In a heat, if there is a tie in the total points given by one or more judges, it shall be broken in favour of the board with the higher single score in the priority category. If the categories are weighted equally, in wave performance competition the tie shall be broken in favour of the board with the higher single score in wave riding, and in freestyle competition in favour of the board with the higher score for overall impression. If a tie remains, in wave performance competition it shall be broken in favour of the board with the higher single score in the category without priority, and in freestyle competition it shall stand as the final result.

(2) If there is a tie in the series score, it shall be broken in favour of the board that scored better more times than the other board. All scores shall be used even if some of them are excluded scores.

(3) If a tie still remains, the heat shall be resailed. If this is not possible, the tie shall stand as the final result.

Appendix BB — Experimental Kiteboard Racing Rules

This appendix is a US SAILING prescription.

A group of race officials and kiteboard racers is developing a set of racing rules to govern 'round the buoys' kiteboard races. These rules are evolving based on the experiences of competitors in kiteboard races and those who serve on the race committee or protest committee at such races. See www.ussailing.org/rules/kiteboards for more information, including the most recent version of these rules.

Appendix C — Match Racing Rules

Match races shall be sailed under The Racing Rules of Sailing *as changed by this appendix. Matches shall be umpired unless the notice of race and sailing instructions state otherwise.*

C1 TERMINOLOGY

'Competitor' means the skipper, team or boat as appropriate for the event. 'Flight' means two or more matches started in the same starting sequence.

C2 CHANGES TO THE DEFINITIONS AND THE RULES OF PARTS 2 AND 4

C2.1 The definition *Finish* is changed to

A boat *finishes* when any part of her hull, or crew or equipment in normal position, crosses the finishing line in the direction of the course from the last *mark* after completing any penalties. However, when penalties are cancelled under rule C7.2(d) after one or both boats have *finished* each shall be recorded as *finished* when she crossed the line.

C2.2 Add to the definition *Proper Course*: 'A boat taking a penalty or manoeuvring to take a penalty is not sailing a *proper course*.'

C2.3 In the definition *Zone* the distance is changed to two hull lengths.

C2.4 Rule 13 is changed to

13 WHILE TACKING OR GYBING

13.1 After a boat passes head to wind, she shall *keep clear* of other boats until she is on a close-hauled course.

13.2 After the foot of the mainsail of a boat sailing downwind crosses the centreline she shall *keep clear* of other boats until her mainsail has filled.

13.3 While rule 13.1 or 13.2 applies, rules 10, 11 and 12 do not. However, if two boats are subject to rule 13.1 or 13.2 at the same time, the one on the other's port side or the one astern shall *keep clear*.

C2.5 Rule 16.2 is deleted.

C2.6 Rule 18.3 is changed to

If two boats were on opposite *tacks* and one of them changes *tack* and as a result is subject to rule 13.1 in the *zone* when the other is *fetching* the *mark*, rule 18.2 does not thereafter apply. If, once the boat that changed *tack* has completed her tack,

(a) the other boat cannot by luffing avoid becoming *overlapped* inside her, she is entitled to *mark-room*, the boat that changed *tack* shall *keep clear* and rule 15 does not apply;

(b) the other boat can by luffing avoid becoming *overlapped* inside her, the boat that changed *tack* is entitled to *mark-room*.

C2.7 When rule 20 applies, the following arm signals by the helmsman are required in addition to the hails:

(a) for 'Room to tack', repeatedly and clearly pointing to windward; and

(b) for 'You tack', repeatedly and clearly pointing at the other boat and waving the arm to windward.

C2.8 Rule 23.1 is changed to 'If reasonably possible, a boat not *racing* shall not interfere with a boat that is *racing* or an umpire boat.'

C2.9 Add new rule 23.3: 'When boats in different matches meet, any change of course by either boat shall be consistent with complying with a *rule* or trying to win her own match.'

C2.10 Add to the preamble of Part 4: 'Rule 42 shall also apply between the warning and preparatory signals.'

C2.11 Rule 42.2(d) is changed to 'sculling: repeated movement of the helm to propel the boat forward;'

C3 RACE SIGNALS AND CHANGES TO RELATED RULES

C3.1 Starting Signals

The signals for starting a match shall be as follows. Times shall be taken from the visual signals; the failure of a sound signal shall be disregarded. If more than one match will be sailed, the starting signal for one match shall be the warning signal for the next match.

Time in minutes	Visual signal	Sound signal	Means
10	Flag F displayed	One	Attention signal
6	Flag F removed	None	
5	Numeral pennant displayed*	One	Warning signal
4	Flag P displayed	One	Preparatory signal
2	Blue or yellow flag or both displayed**	One**	End of pre-start entry time
0	Warning and preparatory signals removed	One	Starting signal

* Within a flight, numeral pennant 1 means Match 1, pennant 2 means Match 2, etc., unless the sailing instructions state otherwise.

** These signals shall be made only if one or both boats fail to comply with rule C4.2. The flag(s) shall be displayed until the umpires have signalled a penalty or for one minute, whichever is earlier.

C3.2 Changes to Related Rules

(a) Rule 29.1 is changed to

(1) When at a boat's starting signal any part of her hull, crew or equipment is on the course side of the starting line or one of its extensions, the race committee shall promptly display a blue or yellow flag identifying the boat with one sound. The flag shall be displayed until the boat is completely on the pre-start side of the starting line or one of its extensions or until two minutes after her starting signal, whichever is earlier.

(2) When at a boat's starting signal no part of her hull, crew or equipment is on the course side of the starting line or one of its extensions, and before she *starts* she sails to the course side across an extension, the race committee shall promptly display a blue or yellow flag identifying the boat. The flag shall be displayed until the

boat is completely on the pre-start side of the start-ing line or one of its extensions or until two minutes after her starting signal, whichever is earlier.

(b) In the race signal AP the last sentence is changed to 'The attention signal will be made 1 minute after removal unless at that time the race is *postponed* again or *abandoned*.'

(c) In the race signal N the last sentence is changed to 'The attention signal will be made 1 minute after removal unless at that time the race is *abandoned* again or *postponed*.'

C3.3 Finishing Line Signals

The race signal Blue flag or shape shall not be used.

C4   REQUIREMENTS BEFORE THE START

C4.1 At her preparatory signal, each boat shall be outside the line that is at a 90° angle to the starting line through the starting *mark* at her assigned end. In the race schedule pairing list, the boat listed on the left-hand side is assigned the port end and shall display a blue flag at her stern while *racing*. The other boat is assigned the starboard end and shall display a yellow flag at her stern while *racing*.

C4.2 Within the two-minute period following her preparatory signal, a boat shall cross and clear the starting line, the first time from the course side to the pre-start side.

C5   SIGNALS BY UMPIRES

C5.1 A green and white flag with one long sound means 'No penalty'.

C5.2 A blue or yellow flag identifying a boat with one long sound means 'The identified boat shall take a penalty by complying with rule C7.'

C5.3 A red flag with or soon after a blue or yellow flag with one long sound means 'The identified boat shall take a penalty by complying with rule C7.3(d).'

C5.4 A black flag with a blue or yellow flag and one long sound means 'The identified boat is disqualified, and the match is terminated and awarded to the other boat.'

C5.5 One short sound means 'A penalty is now completed.'

C5.6 Repetitive short sounds mean 'A boat is no longer taking a penalty and the penalty remains.'

C5.7 A blue or yellow flag or shape displayed from an umpire boat means 'The identified boat has an outstanding penalty.'

C6 PROTESTS AND REQUESTS FOR REDRESS BY BOATS

C6.1 A boat may protest another boat

(a) under a rule of Part 2, except rule 14, by clearly displaying flag Y immediately after an incident in which she was involved;

(b) under any rule not listed in rule C6.1(a) or C6.2 by clearly displaying a red flag as soon as possible after the incident.

C6.2 A boat may not protest another boat under

(a) rule 14, unless damage or injury results;

(b) a rule of Part 2, unless she was involved in the incident;

(c) rule 31 or 42; or

(d) rule C4 or C7.

C6.3 A boat intending to request redress because of circumstances that arise before she *finishes* or retires shall clearly display a red flag as soon as possible after she becomes aware of those circumstances, but no later than two minutes after *finishing* or retiring.

C6.4 (a) A boat protesting under rule C6.1(a) shall remove flag Y before or as soon as possible after the umpires' signal.

(b) A boat protesting under rule C6.1(b) or requesting redress under rule C6.3 shall, for her *protest* or request to be valid, keep her red flag displayed until she has so informed the umpires after *finishing* or retiring. No written *protest* or request for redress is required.

C6.5 Umpire Decisions

(a) After flag Y is displayed, the umpires shall decide whether to penalize any boat. They shall signal their decision in compliance with rule C5.1, C5.2 or C5.3.

(b) The red-flag penalty in rule C5.3 shall be used when a boat has gained a controlling position as a result of breaking a *rule*, but the umpires are not certain that the conditions for an additional umpire-initiated penalty have been fulfilled.

C6.6 Protest Committee Decisions

(a) The protest committee may take evidence in any way it considers appropriate and may communicate its decision orally.

(b) If the protest committee decides that a breach of a *rule* has had no significant effect on the outcome of the match, it may

    (1) impose a penalty of one point or part of one point;

    (2) order a resail; or

    (3) make another arrangement it decides is equitable, which may be to impose no penalty.

(c) The penalty for breaking rule 14 when damage or injury results will be at the discretion of the protest committee, and may include exclusion from further races in the event.

C7 PENALTY SYSTEM

C7.1 Deleted Rule

Rule 44 is deleted.

C7.2 All Penalties

(a) A penalized boat may delay taking a penalty within the limitations of rule C7.3 and shall take it as follows:

    (1) When on a leg of the course to a windward *mark*, she shall gybe and, as soon as reasonably possible, luff to a close-hauled course.

    (2) When on a leg of the course to a leeward *mark* or the finishing line, she shall tack and, as soon as reasonably possible, bear away to a course that is more than ninety degrees from the true wind.

(b) Add to rule 2: 'When *racing*, a boat need not take a penalty unless signalled to do so by an umpire.'

(c) A boat completes a leg of the course when her bow crosses the extension of the line from the previous *mark* through the *mark* she is rounding, or on the last leg when she *finishes*.

(d) A penalized boat shall not be recorded as having *finished* until she takes her penalty and sails completely to the course side of the line and then *finishes*, unless the penalty is cancelled before or after she crosses the finishing line.

(e) If a boat has one or two outstanding penalties and the other boat in her match is penalized, one penalty for each boat shall be cancelled except that a red-flag penalty shall not cancel or be cancelled by another penalty.

(f) If a boat has more than two outstanding penalties, the umpires shall signal her disqualification under rule C5.4.

C7.3 Penalty Limitations

(a) A boat taking a penalty that includes a tack shall have the spinnaker head below the main-boom gooseneck from the time she passes head to wind until she is on a close-hauled course.

(b) No part of a penalty may be taken inside the *zone* of a rounding *mark* that begins, bounds or ends the leg the boat is on.

(c) If a boat has one outstanding penalty, she may take the penalty any time after *starting* and before *finishing*. If a boat has two outstanding penalties, she shall take one of them as soon as reasonably possible, but not before *starting*.

(d) When the umpires display a red flag with or soon after a penalty flag, the penalized boat shall take a penalty as soon as reasonably possible, but not before *starting*.

C7.4 Taking and Completing Penalties

(a) When a boat with an outstanding penalty is on a leg to a windward *mark* and gybes, or is on a leg to a lee-ward *mark* or the finishing line and passes head to wind, she is taking a penalty.

(b) When a boat taking a penalty either does not take the penalty correctly or does not complete the penalty as soon as reasonably possible, she is no longer taking a penalty. The umpires shall signal this as required by rule C5.6.

(c) The umpire boat for each match shall display blue or yellow flags or shapes, each flag or shape indicating one outstanding penalty. When a boat has taken a penalty, or a penalty has been cancelled, one flag or shape shall be removed. Failure of the umpires to display or remove flags or shapes shall not change the number of penalties outstanding.

C8   PENALTIES INITIATED BY UMPIRES

C8.1   Rule Changes

(a)   Rules 60.2(a) and 60.3(a) do not apply to *rules* for which penalties may be imposed by umpires.

(b)   Rule 64.1(c) is changed so that the provision for exonerating a boat may be applied by the umpires without a hearing, and it takes precedence over any conflicting rule of this appendix.

C8.2   When the umpires decide that a boat has broken rule 31, 42, C4, C7.3(c) or C7.3(d) she shall be penalized by signalling her under rule C5.2 or C5.3. However, if a boat is penalized for breaking a rule of Part 2 and if she in the same incident breaks rule 31, she shall not be penalized for breaking rule 31. Furthermore, a boat that displays an incorrect flag or does not display the correct flag shall be warned orally and given an opportunity to correct the error before being penalized.

C8.3   When the umpires decide that a boat has

(a)   gained an advantage by breaking a *rule* after allowing for a penalty,

(b)   deliberately broken a *rule*, or

(c)   committed a breach of sportsmanship,

she shall be penalized under rule C5.2, C5.3 or C5.4.

C8.4   If the umpires or protest committee members decide that a boat may have broken a *rule* other than those listed in rules C6.1(a) and C6.2, they shall so inform the protest committee for its action under rule 60.3 and rule C6.6 when appropriate.

C8.5   When, after one boat has *started*, the umpires are satisfied that the other boat will not *start*, they may signal under rule C5.4 that the boat that did not *start* is disqualified and the match is terminated.

C8.6   When the match umpires, together with at least one other umpire, decide that a boat has broken rule 14 and damage resulted, they may impose a half-point penalty without a hearing. The competitor shall be informed of the penalty as soon as practicable and may request a hearing. The protest committee shall then proceed under rule C6.6. Any penalty decided by the protest committee may be more than half a point. When the umpires decide that a penalty greater than half a point is appropriate, they shall act under rule C8.4.

C9 REQUESTS FOR REDRESS OR REOPENING; APPEALS; OTHER PROCEEDINGS

C9.1 There shall be no request for redress or an appeal from a decision made under rule C5, C6, C7 or C8. In rule 66 the third sentence is changed to 'A *party* to the hearing may not ask for a reopening.'

C9.2 A competitor may not base a request for redress on a claim that an action by an official boat was improper. The protest committee may decide to consider giving redress in such circumstances but only if it believes that an official boat, including an umpire boat, may have seriously interfered with a competing boat.

C9.3 No proceedings of any kind may be taken in relation to any action or non-action by the umpires, except as permitted in rule C9.2.

C10 SCORING

C10.1 The winning competitor of each match scores one point (half a point each for a dead heat); the loser scores no points.

C10.2 When a competitor withdraws from part of an event the scores of all completed races shall stand.

C10.3 When a multiple round robin is terminated with an incomplete round robin, only one point shall be available for all the matches sailed between any two competitors, as follows:

Number of matches completed between any two competitors	Points for each win
1	One point
2	Half a point
3	A third of a point
(etc.)	

C10.4 In a round-robin series,

(a) competitors shall be placed in order of their total scores, highest score first;

  (b) a competitor who has won a match but is disqualified
      for breaking a *rule* against a competitor in another
      match shall lose the point for that match (but the los-
      ing competitor shall not be awarded the point); and

  (c) the overall position between competitors who have
      sailed in different groups shall be decided by the
      highest score.

C10.5 In a knockout series the sailing instructions shall state
the minimum number of points required to win a series
between two competitors. When a knockout series is terminated it shall be decided in favour of the competitor
with the higher score.

C11 TIES

C11.1 Round-Robin Series

*In a round-robin series competitors are assigned to one or
more groups and scheduled to sail against all other competitors in their group one or more times. Each separate
stage identified in the event format shall be a separate
round-robin series irrespective of the number of times
each competitor sails against each other competitor
in that stage.*

Ties between two or more competitors in a round-robin
series shall be broken by the following methods, in order,
until all ties are broken. When one or more ties are only
partially broken, rules C11.1(a) to C11.1(e) shall be reap-
plied to them. Ties shall be decided in favour of the
competitor(s) who

  (a) placed in order, has the highest score in the matches
      between the tied competitors;

  (b) when the tie is between two competitors in a multiple
      round robin, has won the last match between the two
      competitors;

  (c) has the most points against the competitor placed high-
      est in the round-robin series or, if necessary, second
      highest, and so on until the tie is broken. When two
      separate ties have to be resolved but the resolution of
      each depends upon resolving the other, the following
      principles shall be used in the rule C11.1(c) procedure:

      (1) the higher-place tie shall be resolved before the
          lower-place tie, and

(2) all the competitors in the lower-place tie shall be treated as a single competitor for the purposes of rule C11.1(c);

(d) after applying rule C10.4(c), has the highest place in the different groups, irrespective of the number of competitors in each group;

(e) has the highest place in the most recent stage of the event (fleet race, round robin, etc.).

C11.2 Knockout Series

Ties (including 0–0) between competitors in a knockout series shall be broken by the following methods, in order, until the tie is broken. The tie shall be decided in favour of the competitor who

(a) has the highest place in the most recent round-robin series, applying rule C11.1 if necessary;

(b) has won the most recent match in the event between the tied competitors.

C11.3 Remaining Ties

When rule C11.1 or C11.2 does not resolve a tie,

(a) if the tie needs to be resolved for a later stage of the event (or another event for which the event is a direct qualifier), the tie shall be broken by a sail-off when practicable. When the race committee decides that a sail-off is not practicable, the tie shall be decided in favour of the competitor who has the highest score in the round-robin series after eliminating the score for the first race for each tied competitor or, should this fail to break the tie, the second race for each tied competitor and so on until the tie is broken. When a tie is partially resolved, the remaining tie shall be broken by reapplying rule C11.1 or C11.2.

(b) to decide the winner of an event that is not a direct qualifier for another event, or the overall position between competitors eliminated in one round of a knockout series, a sail-off may be used (but not a draw).

(c) when a tie is not broken any monetary prizes or ranking points for tied places shall be added together and divided equally among the tied competitors.

Note: A Standard Notice of Race and Standard Sailing Instructions for match racing are available from the ISAF.

Appendix D — Team Racing Rules

Team races shall be sailed under The Racing Rules of Sailing *as changed by this appendix. If umpires will be used the sailing instructions shall so state.*

D1 CHANGES TO THE RACING RULES

D1.1 Changes to the Definitions and the Rules of Part 2

(a) In the definition *Zone* the distance is changed to two hull lengths.

(b) The second sentence of rule 18.2(b) is changed to 'If a boat is *clear ahead* when she reaches the *zone*, or she later becomes *clear ahead* when another boat passes head to wind, the boat *clear astern* at that moment shall thereafter give her *mark-room*.'

(c) Rule 18.4 is deleted.

(d) Add new rule 23.3: 'A boat that has *finished* shall not act to interfere with a boat that has not *finished*.'

(e) Add new rule 23.4: 'When boats in different races meet, any change of course by either boat shall be consistent with complying with a *rule* or trying to win her own race.'

D1.2 Other Additional Rules

(a) There shall be no penalty for breaking a rule of Part 2 when the incident is between boats on the same team and there is no contact.

(b) Add to rule 41: 'However, a boat may receive help from another boat on her team provided electronic communication is not used.'

(c) A boat is not eligible for redress based on damage or injury caused by another boat on her team.

(d) The first sentence of rule 45 is deleted.

D2 PROTESTS AND PENALTIES

D2.1 Protests and Exoneration

(a) Rule 60.1(a) is changed to 'protest another boat, but not for an alleged breach of a rule of Part 2 unless she was involved in the incident or the incident involved contact between members of the other team; or'.

(b) The third sentence of rule 61.1(a) and all of rule 61.1(a)(2) are deleted.

(c) A boat that, while *racing*, may have broken a rule of Part 2 (except rule 14 when she has caused damage or injury) or rule 42 may take a One-Turn Penalty under rule 44.2.

d) The sailing instructions may state that rule D2.4(b) applies to all *protests*.

D2.2 Umpired Races

Races to be umpired shall be identified either in the sailing instructions or by the display of flag U no later than the warning signal.

(a) When a boat protests under a rule of Part 2 or under rule 31, 42 or 44, she is not entitled to a hearing. Instead, when the protested boat fails either to acknowledge breaking a *rule* or to take the appropriate penalty, the protesting boat may request a decision by conspicuously displaying a yellow flag and hailing 'Umpire'.

(b) An umpire shall signal a decision as follows:

(1) A green and white flag or a green flag means 'No penalty'.

(2) A red flag means 'One or more boats are penalized.' The umpire shall hail or signal to identify each boat to be penalized.

(c) A boat penalized under rule D2.2(b)(2) shall take a Two-Turns Penalty under rule 44.2.

(d) PENALTIES INITIATED BY UMPIRES

An umpire may take action without a *protest* by another boat when

(1) a boat breaks rule 31 or 42, or a rule of Part 2 through contact with another boat on her team, and does not take a penalty;

(2) a boat fails to comply with rule D2.2(c);

(3) a boat commits a breach of sportsmanship;

(4) a boat breaks rule 14 when damage or injury may have been caused; or

(5) a boat or her team gains an advantage despite taking a penalty.

The umpire may impose a penalty of one or more turns, each including one tack and one gybe, signalled by displaying a red flag and hailing the boat accordingly, or report the incident to the protest committee, signalled by displaying a black flag, or both.

D2.3 Alternative Umpiring Rules

Each of these rules applies only if the sailing instructions so state.

(a) SINGLE-FLAG PROTEST PROCEDURE

Rule D2.2(a) is replaced by

When a boat protests under a rule of Part 2 or under rule 31, 42 or 44, she is not entitled to a hearing. Instead, a boat involved in the incident may promptly acknowledge breaking a *rule* and take the appropriate penalty. If no boat takes a penalty, an umpire shall decide whether any boat has broken a *rule*, and shall signal the decision in compliance with rule D2.2(b).

(b) RACES WITH LIMITED UMPIRING

Rule D2.2 applies, except that when a boat complies with rule D2.2(a) and either there is no decision signalled or an umpire displays a yellow flag signalling he has insufficient facts to decide, the protesting boat is entitled to a hearing.

D2.4 Additional Protest and Redress Rules When Races Are Umpired

(a) Neither the race committee nor the protest committee shall protest a boat for breaking a rule listed in rule D2.2(a). However, upon receipt of a report from any source, the protest committee may protest a boat under rule 14 when damage or injury is alleged.

(b) *Protests* and requests for redress need not be in writing. The protest committee may take evidence in any way it considers appropriate and may communicate its decision orally.

(c) There shall be no request for redress or appeal by a boat arising from a decision, action or non-action by an umpire. The protest committee may decide to consider giving redress when it believes that an official boat, including an umpire boat, may have seriously interfered with a competing boat.

D3   SCORING A RACE

D3.1 (a) Each boat *finishing* a race, whether or not rule 28.1 has been complied with, shall be scored points equal to her finishing place. All other boats shall be scored points equal to the number of boats entitled to *race*.

(b) In addition, a boat's points shall be increased as follows:

Rule broken	Penalty points
Rule 28.1 when as a result she or her team has gained an advantage	10
Any other *rule* broken while *racing* for which a penalty has not been taken	6

(c) After a hearing the protest committee may penalize as follows:

    (1) When a boat has broken a *rule* and as a result her team has gained an advantage, it may increase that boat's points.

    (2) When a boat has broken rule 1 or 2, rule 14 when she has caused damage or injury, or a *rule* when not *racing*, it may penalize the boat's team by half or more race wins, or it may impose no penalty.

(d) The team with the lower total points wins the race. If the totals are equal, the team that did not have the first-place boat wins.

D3.2 When all boats on one team have *finished*, retired or failed to *start*, the race committee may stop the race. The other team's boats *racing* at that time shall be scored the points they would have received had they *finished*.

D4   SCORING A SERIES

D4.1 When two or more teams are competing in a series, the winner shall be the team scoring the greatest number of race wins. The other teams shall be ranked in order of number of race wins.

D4.2 When necessary, ties in a completed series shall be broken using, in order,

    (a) the number of races won when the tied teams met;

    (b) the points scored when the tied teams met;

    (c) if two teams remain tied, the last race between them;

    (d) total points scored in all races against common opponents;

    (e) a sail-off if possible, otherwise a game of chance.

If a tie is partially resolved by one of these, then the remaining tie shall be broken by starting again at rule D4.2(a).

D4.3 If a series is not completed, teams shall be ranked according to the results from completed rounds, and ties shall be broken whenever possible using the results from races between the tied teams in the incomplete round. If no round has been completed, teams shall be ranked in order of their percentages of races won. Other ties shall be broken as provided in rule D4.2.

D5 BREAKDOWNS WHEN BOATS ARE SUPPLIED BY THE ORGANIZING AUTHORITY

D5.1 A supplied boat suffering a breakdown, and seeking redress as a result, shall display a red flag at the first reasonable opportunity and, if possible, continue *racing*. The race committee shall decide redress as provided in rules D5.2 and D5.3.

D5.2 When the race committee decides that the boat's finishing position was made significantly worse, that the breakdown was through no fault of the crew, and that in the same circumstances a reasonably competent crew would not have been able to avoid the breakdown, it shall make as equitable a decision as possible. This may be to order the race to be resailed or, when the boat's finishing position was predictable, award her points for that position. Any doubt about a boat's position when she broke down shall be resolved against her.

D5.3 A breakdown caused by defective supplied equipment or a breach of a *rule* by an opponent shall not normally be determined to be the fault of the crew, but one caused by careless handling, capsizing or a breach by a boat on the same team shall be. Any doubt about the fault of the crew shall be resolved in the boat's favour.

Appendix E — Radio-Controlled Boat Racing Rules

Races for radio-controlled boats shall be sailed under The Racing Rules of Sailing *as changed by this appendix.*

E1 TERMINOLOGY, RACE SIGNALS, DEFINITIONS AND FUNDAMENTAL RULES

E1.1 Terminology

'Boat' means a boat that is radio-controlled by a competitor who is not on board. For 'race' used as a noun outside this appendix and outside Appendix A read 'heat'. In this appendix, a race consists of one or more heats and is completed when the last heat in the race is finished. An 'event' consists of one or more races.

E1.2 Race Signals

The section Race Signals is deleted. All signals shall be made orally or by other sounds described in this appendix or the sailing instructions.

E1.3 Definitions

(a) Add to the definition *Interested Party*: 'but not a competitor when acting as an observer'.

(b) In the definition *Zone* the distance is changed to four hull lengths.

E1.4 Personal Flotation Devices

Rule 1.2 is changed to 'When on board a rescue boat, each competitor is responsible for wearing a personal flotation device adequate for the conditions.'

E1.5 Aerials

Transmitter aerial extremities shall be adequately protected. When a protest committee finds that a competitor has broken this rule it shall either warn him and give him time to comply or penalize him.

E2 PART 2 WHEN BOATS MEET

Rule 22 is changed to

22 CAPSIZED OR ENTANGLED

If possible, a boat shall avoid a boat that is capsized or entangled, or has not regained control after capsizing or entanglement. A boat is capsized when her masthead is in the water. Two or more boats are entangled when lying together for a period of

time so that no boat is capable of manoeuvring to
break free of the other(s).

E3   PART 3   CONDUCT OF A RACE

E3.1   Races with Observers

The race committee may appoint race observers, who
may be competitors. They shall remain in the control area
while boats are *racing* and they shall hail and repeat the
identity of boats that contact a *mark* or another boat. Such
hails shall be made from the control area. Observers shall
report all unresolved incidents to the race committee at
the end of the heat.

E3.2   Course Board

Rule J2.1(4) is deleted. A course board showing the
course and the limits of the control area and launching
area(s) shall be located next to or within the control area
with information clearly visible to competitors while *racing*.

E3.3   Control and Launching Areas

The control and launching area(s) shall be defined by the
sailing instructions. Competitors *racing* shall remain in the
control area while a heat is in progress, except that competitors may briefly go to and return from the launching
area to perform functions permitted in rule E4.5. Competitors not *racing* shall remain outside the control and
launching areas except when offering assistance under
rule E4.2 or when acting as race observers.

E3.4   Deleted Rules

The second sentence of rule 25 and all of rule 33 are
deleted.

E3.5   Starting Races

Rule 26 is changed to

> Audible signals for starting a heat shall be at one-
> minute intervals and shall be a warning signal, a
> preparatory signal and a starting signal. During the
> minute before the starting signal, oral signals shall
> be made at ten-second intervals, and during the final
> ten seconds at one-second intervals. Each signal
> shall be timed from the beginning of its sound.

E3.6   Starting Penalties

In rules 29.1 and 30 the word 'crew' is deleted. Throughout rule 30 oral announcements shall be used instead of flag signals.

E3.7 Starting and Finishing Lines

The starting and finishing lines shall be tangential to, and on the course side of, the starting and finishing *marks*.

E3.8 Individual Recall

In rule 29.1 replace all after 'the race committee shall promptly' with 'twice hail "Recall (sail numbers)" '.

E3.9 General Recall

In rule 29.2 replace all after 'the race committee may' with 'twice hail "General recall" and make two loud sounds. The warning signal for a new start for the recalled class shall be made shortly thereafter, and the starts for any succeeding classes shall follow the new start.'

E3.10 Shortening or Abandoning after the Start

In rule 32.1(b) 'foul weather' is replaced with 'thunder-storms'. Rule 32.1(c) is deleted.

E4   PART 4   OTHER REQUIREMENTS WHEN RACING

E4.1 Deleted Rules

Rules 43, 47, 48, 49, 50, 52 and 54 are deleted.

E4.2 Outside Help

Rule 41 is changed to

(a) A competitor shall not give tactical or strategic advice to a competitor who is *racing*.

(b) A competitor who is *racing* shall not receive outside help, except

(1) a boat that has gone ashore or aground outside the launching area, or become entangled with another boat or a *mark*, may be freed and re-launched with help from a rescue boat crew;

(2) competitors who are not *racing* and others may give help in the launching area as permitted by rule E4.5;

(3) help in the form of information freely available to all competitors.

E4.3 Propulsion

Rule 42 is changed so that any reference to body move-ment is deleted. Rule 42.3(f) is also deleted.

E4.4 Penalties for Breaking Rules of Part 2

Throughout rule 44 the penalty shall be the One-Turn Penalty.

E4.5 Launching and Relaunching

Rule 45 is changed to

(a) A boat scheduled to *race* in a heat may be launched, held on the bank, taken ashore or relaunched at any time during the heat. However, she shall not be released between the preparatory and starting signals.

(b) Boats shall be launched or recovered only from within a launching area, except as provided in rule E4.2(b)(1).

(c) While ashore or within a launching area, boats may be adjusted, drained of water or repaired; have their sails changed or reefed; have entangled objects removed; or have radio equipment repaired or changed.

E4.6 Person in Charge

In rule 46 replace 'have on board' with 'be radio-controlled by'.

E4.7 Radio

(a) A competitor shall not transmit radio signals that cause interference with the radio reception of other boats.

(b) A competitor found to have broken rule E4.7(a) shall not *race* until he has proven compliance with that rule.

E4.8 Boat Out of Radio Control

A competitor who loses radio control of his boat shall promptly hail and repeat '(The boat's sail number) out of control'. Such a boat shall be considered to have retired and shall thereafter be an *obstruction*.

E5 PART 5 PROTESTS, REDRESS, HEARINGS, MISCONDUCT AND APPEALS

E5.1 Right to Protest; Right to Request Redress or Rule 69 Action

Add to rule 60.1(a): 'A *protest* alleging a breach of a rule of Part 2, 3 or 4 shall be made only by a competitor within the control or launching area and by a boat scheduled to *race* in the heat in which the incident occurred.'

E5.2 Informing the Protestee

In rule 61.1(a) replace all after the first sentence with 'When her *protest* concerns an incident in the racing area that she is involved in or sees, she shall twice hail "(Her own sail number) protest (the sail number of the other boat)".'

E5.3 Protest Time Limit

In rule 61.3 replace 'two hours' with '15 minutes' and add: 'A boat intending to protest shall also inform the race committee no later than five minutes after the end of the relevant heat.'

E5.4 Accepting Responsibility

A boat that acknowledges breaking a rule of Part 2, 3 or 4 before the *protest* is found to be valid may retire from the relevant heat without further penalty.

E5.5 Redress

(a) Add to rule 62.1:
  (e) radio interference, or
  (f) an entanglement or grounding because of the action of a boat that was breaking a rule of Part 2 or of a vessel not *racing* that was required to keep clear.

(b) In rule 62.2 replace 'two hours' with '15 minutes'.

E5.6 Right to Be Present

In rule 63.3(a) replace 'shall have been on board' with 'shall have been radio-controlling them'.

E5.7 Taking Evidence and Finding Facts

Add to rule 63.6: 'Evidence about an alleged breach of a rule of Part 2, 3 or 4 given by competitors shall be accepted only from a competitor who was within the control or launching area and whose boat was scheduled to *race* in the heat in which the incident occurred.'

E5.8 Penalties

When a protest committee finds that a boat has broken rule E3.3, E4.2(a) or E4.5, it shall either disqualify her from her next race or require her to make one or more penalty turns in her next race as soon as possible after *starting*.

E5.9 Decisions on Redress

Add to rule 64.2: 'If a boat given redress was damaged, she shall be given reasonable time, but not more than 30 minutes, to effect repairs before her next heat.'

E5.10 Reopening a Hearing

In rule 66 replace '24 hours' with 'ten minutes'.

E6   APPENDIX G   IDENTIFICATION ON SAILS

Appendix G is changed as follows:

(a) The text of rule G1.1 before rule G1.1(a) is changed to
     Every boat of a class administered by ISAF Radio Con-
     trolled Sailing shall display a sail number on both sides
     of each sail. Class insignia and national letters shall
     be displayed on mainsails as stated in rules G1.1(a),
     G1.1(b) and E6(f)(1).

(b) Rule G1.1(c) is changed to
     a sail number, which shall be the last two digits of the
     boat registration number or the competitor's personal
     number allotted by the relevant issuing authority. A
     single-digit number shall be prefixed with a '0'. There
     shall be space in front of a sail number for the prefix '1',
     which may be required by the race committee where
     there is a conflict between sail numbers. Where a con-
     flict remains, the race committee shall require that
     sail numbers be suitably changed until the conflict
     is resolved. Any prefix '1' or other required change
     shall become part of the sail number.

(c) The sentence after rule G1.1(c) is deleted.

(d) Rule G1.2(b) is changed to
     The height of characters and distance between them
     on the same and opposite sides of the sail shall be as
     follows:

	Minimum	Maximum
Class insignia:		
Except where positioned back to back, shortest distance between insignia on opposite sides of sail	20 mm	
Sail numbers:		
Height of characters	100 mm	110 mm
Shortest distance between adjoining characters on same side of sail	20 mm	30 mm

	Minimum	Maximum
Shortest distance between sail numbers on opposite sides of sail and between sail numbers and other identification	60 mm	
National letters:		
Height of characters	60 mm	70 mm
Shortest distance between adjoining characters on same side of sail	13 mm	23 mm
Shortest distance between national letters on opposite sides of sail	40 mm	

(e) Rule G1.3 is changed to
  (1) Class insignia may be positioned back to back on opposite sides of the sail where the design coincides. Otherwise class insignia, sail numbers and national letters shall be positioned at different heights, with those on the starboard side being uppermost.
  (2) On a mainsail, sail numbers shall be positioned above the national letters and below the class insignia.
  (3) Sail numbers shall be positioned on a mainsail above the line perpendicular to the luff through the quarter leech point.
(f) Where the size of a sail makes it impossible to comply with the minimum dimensions in rule E6(d) or the positioning requirements in rule E6(e)(3), exceptions are permitted in the following order of priority:
  (1) omission of national letters;
  (2) position of the mainsail sail numbers lower than the line perpendicular to the luff through the quarter leech point;
  (3) reduction of the shortest distance between sail numbers on opposite sides of the sail provided the shortest distance is not less than 20 mm;
  (4) reduction of the height of sail numbers.

Appendix F — Procedures for Appeals and Requests

This appendix is a US SAILING prescription.
See rules 70 and 71. This appendix replaces Appendix F as adopted by the International Sailing Federation. The US SAILING Appeals Committee acts as the national authority within the meaning of rules 70.1 and 71.

F1 WHERE TO SEND AN APPEAL OR REQUEST

F1.1 All appeals and requests shall be sent to the Race Administration Director at US SAILING, at either P.O. Box 1260 or 15 Maritime Drive, Portsmouth, RI 02871, or by e-mail to RaceAdmin@ussailing.org.

F1.2 Except as provided in rule F1.4, the director will forward an appeal of a decision of a protest committee or a request by a protest committee for confirmation or correction of its decision to the association appeals committee for the place in which the event was held. However, such an appeal or request arising from an event conducted under the procedural rules of the Intercollegiate Sailing Association or the Interscholastic Sailing Association will be forwarded to the association appeals committee for the ICSA and ISSA.

F1.3 The director will forward an appeal of a decision of an association appeals committee, a request by an association appeals committee for confirmation or correction of its decision, and a request for an interpretation of *rules* to the US SAILING Appeals Committee.

F1.4 The director will forward an appeal of a decision of a protest committee acting under rule 69.1, an appeal of a decision of a protest committee of a US SAILING national championship, and a request by such a committee for confirmation or correction of its decision to the US SAILING Appeals Committee.

F2 TO APPEAL OR MAKE A REQUEST

F2.1 To appeal the decision of a protest committee or association appeals committee a *party* to the hearing shall, no later than 15 days after receiving the written decision being appealed or a protest committee's decision not to reopen a hearing, send an appeal and a copy of the decision to the US SAILING Race Administration Director. The appeal shall state why the appellant believes the committee's decision or its procedures were incorrect.

F2.2   The appellant shall also send, with the appeal or as soon as possible thereafter, all of the following documents that are available:

   (a)   the written *protest*(s) or request(s) for redress;

   (b)   if the appeal is from a decision of an association appeals committee, the written decision of the protest committee;

   (c)   a diagram, prepared or endorsed by the protest committee, that shows

   (1)   the positions of all boats involved at relevant times, and their tracks;

   (2)   the course to the next *mark* and its required side;

   (3)   the speed and direction of the wind;

   (4)   any relevant *mark*, *obstruction* or *zone*; and

   (5)   if relevant, the depth of the water and the speed and direction of any current;

   (d)   the notice of race, sailing instructions, any other documents governing the event, and any changes to them;

   (e)   the names, mailing addresses and e-mail addresses of the *parties* to the hearing, the chairman of the protest committee and, if relevant, the chairman of the association appeals committee; and

   (f)   any other relevant documents.

F2.3   To request confirmation or correction of its decision, a protest committee or association appeals committee shall send to the US SAILING Race Administration Director a copy of its decision and all relevant documents and comments.

F2.4   To request an interpretation of the *rules*, a club or other organization affiliated to US SAILING shall send to the US SAILING Race Administration Director its request, which shall include assumed facts. A US SAILING committee is considered to be an organization affiliated to US SAILING.

F3   **FEES**

F3.1   If a fee is required for an appeal or request, it must be received before the appeal or request will be considered.

F3.2   US SAILING charges no fee for forwarding an appeal or request to an association appeals committee. However, the association appeals committee may charge a fee. In that case, the association appeals committee will send a notice to the appellant (or, for a request, to the protest committee) stating the fee, to whom the fee is payable, and the address to which the fee must be sent.

F3.3 US SAILING charges a fee of $25 for an appeal made to the US SAILING Appeals Committee (see rules F1.3 and F1.4) by a member of US SAILING or another national authority. The fee is $75 for all others. A fee of $25 is charged for a request for an interpretation of the rules, but there is no fee for a request from a US SAILING committee. There is no fee for a request from an association appeals committee for confirmation or correction of its decision.

F4 NOTIFICATION OF THE COMMITTEE WHOSE DECISION IS BEING APPEALED

Upon receipt of an appeal, the appeals committee shall send a copy of the appeal to the committee whose decision is being appealed, asking it for any documents required by rule F2.2 not supplied by the appellant.

F5 COMMITTEE RESPONSIBILITIES

F5.1 Protest Committee

A protest committee whose decision is being appealed shall supply the documents requested under rule F4 and any facts or other information requested under rule F6. If directed to do so by the appeals committee, it shall conduct a hearing, or reopen the hearing, of the *protest* or request for redress, or conduct a hearing to consider redress.

F5.2 Association Appeals Committee

(a) The association appeals committee shall send to all *parties* to the hearing, and to the committee whose decision is being appealed or reviewed, copies of all relevant documents and comments it has received, except those supplied by that *party* or committee.

(b) The association appeals committee shall send its decision in writing to all *parties* to the hearing and the protest committee.

(c) An association appeals committee shall consider an appeal it has refused to decide if directed to do so by the US SAILING Appeals Committee.

F5.3 US SAILING Appeals Committee

The US SAILING Appeals Committee shall send to all *parties* to the hearing, to the protest committee and to the association appeals committee whose decision is being appealed or reviewed, copies of all relevant documents and comments it has received, except those supplied by that *party* or committee.

F6 INADEQUATE FACTS; REOPENING

An appeals committee shall accept the protest committee's finding of facts except when it decides they are inadequate. In that case it shall require the protest committee to provide additional facts or other information, or to reopen the hearing and report any new finding of facts, and the protest committee shall promptly do so.

F7 COMMENTS

The *parties* to the hearing, the protest committee and, if relevant, the association appeals committee may make comments on the appeal or request or on any of the documents listed in rule F2.2. Comments shall be sent in writing to the appeals committee no later than 15 days after the *party* or committee receives the document. The appeals committee need not consider comments sent after that time.

F8 OTHER PROVISIONS

These provisions are in addition to those of rule 71.

(a) An association appeals committee may act as permitted by rule 71.2 and shall act as required by rule 71.3, subject to further appeal as provided in rule F1.3.

(b) An association appeals committee may request confirmation or correction of its decision (see rules F1.3 and F2.3).

(c) An appeals committee may direct a protest committee to conduct a hearing to consider redress for an appellant or other *party* to the hearing.

(d) No member of the association appeals committee shall take part in the discussion or decision on an appeal or a request for confirmation or correction to the US SAILING Appeals Committee.

(e) The US SAILING Appeals Committee may direct an association appeals committee to consider an appeal it has refused to decide.

Appendix G — Identification on Sails

See rule 77.

G1 **ISAF INTERNATIONAL CLASS BOATS**

G1.1 **Identification**

Every boat of an ISAF International Class or Recognized Class shall carry on her mainsail and, as provided in rules G1.3(d) and G1.3(e) for letters and numbers only, on her spinnaker and headsail

(a) the insignia denoting her class;

(b) at all international events, except when the boats are provided to all competitors, national letters denoting her national authority from the table below. For the purposes of this rule, international events are ISAF events, world and continental championships, and events described as international events in their notices of race and sailing instructions; and

(c) a sail number of no more than four digits allotted by her national authority or, when so required by the class rules, by the international class association. The four-digit limitation does not apply to classes whose ISAF membership or recognition took effect before 1 April 1997. Alternatively, if permitted in the class rules, an owner may be allotted a personal sail number by the relevant issuing authority, which may be used on all his boats in that class.

Sails measured before 31 March 1999 shall comply with rule G1.1 or with the rules applicable at the time of measurement.

NATIONAL SAIL LETTERS

National authority	Letters	National authority	Letters
Algeria	ALG	Bahamas	BAH
American Samoa	ASA	Bahrain	BRN
Andorra	AND	Barbados	BAR
Angola	ANG	Belarus	BLR
Antigua	ANT	Belgium	BEL
Argentina	ARG	Bermuda	BER
Armenia	ARM	Brazil	BRA
Australia	AUS	British Virgin Islands	IVB
Austria	AUT	Bulgaria	BUL
Azerbaijan	AZE	Canada	CAN

National authority	Letters	National authority	Letters
Cayman Islands	CAY	Kuwait	KUW
Chile	CHI	Kyrgyzstan	KGZ
China, PR	CHN	Latvia	LAT
Chinese Taipei	TPE	Lebanon	LIB
Colombia	COL	Libya	LBA
Cook Islands	COK	Liechtenstein	LIE
Croatia	CRO	Lithuania	LTU
Cuba	CUB	Luxembourg	LUX
Cyprus	CYP	Macedonia (FYRO)	MKD
Czech Republic	CZE	Malaysia	MAS
Denmark	DEN	Malta	MLT
Dominican Republic	DOM	Mauritius	MRI
Ecuador	ECU	Mexico	MEX
Egypt	EGY	Micronesia (FSo)	FSM
El Salvador	ESA	Moldova	MDA
Estonia	EST	Monaco	MON
Fiji	FIJ	Montenegro	MNE
Finland	FIN	Morocco	MAR
France	FRA	Myanmar	MYA
Georgia	GEO	Namibia	NAM
Germany	GER	Netherlands	NED
Great Britain	GBR	Netherlands Antilles	AHO
Greece	GRE	New Zealand	NZL
Grenada	GRN	Norway	NOR
Guam	GUM	Oman	OMA
Guatemala	GUA	Pakistan	PAK
Hong Kong	HKG	Palestine	PLE
Hungary	HUN	Papua New Guinea	PNG
Iceland	ISL	Paraguay	PAR
India	IND	Peru	PER
Indonesia	INA	Philippines	PHI
Ireland	IRL	Poland	POL
Israel	ISR	Portugal	POR
Italy	ITA	Puerto Rico	PUR
Jamaica	JAM	Qatar	QAT
Japan	JPN	Romania	ROU
Kazakhstan	KAZ	Russia	RUS
Kenya	KEN	Samoa	SAM
Korea	KOR	San Marino	SMR

National authority	Letters	National authority	Letters
Senegal	SEN	Thailand	THA
Serbia	SRB	Trinidad & Tobago	TRI
Seychelles	SEY	Tunisia	TUN
Singapore	SIN	Turkey	TUR
Slovak Republic	SVK	Ukraine	UKR
Slovenia	SLO	United Arab	UAE
Solomon Islands	SOL	Emirates	
South Africa	RSA	United States	USA
Spain	ESP	of America	
Sri Lanka	SRI	Uruguay	URU
St Lucia	LCA	US Virgin Islands	ISV
Sweden	SWE	Vanuatu	VAN
Switzerland	SUI	Venezuela	VEN
Tahiti	TAH	Zimbabwe	ZIM

Note: An up-to-date list is available on the ISAF website.

G1.2 Specifications

(a) National letters and sail numbers shall be in capital letters and Arabic numerals, clearly legible and of the same colour. Commercially available typefaces giving the same or better legibility than Helvetica are acceptable.

(b) The height of characters and space between adjoining characters on the same and opposite sides of the sail shall be related to the boat's overall length as follows:

Overall length	Minimum height	Minimum space between characters and from edge of sail
under 3.5 m	230 mm	45 mm
3.5 m – 8.5 m	300 mm	60 mm
8.5 m – 11 m	375 mm	75 mm
over 11 m	450 mm	90 mm

G1.3 Positioning

Class insignia, national letters and sail numbers shall be positioned as follows:

(a) Except as provided in rules G1.3(d) and G1.3(e), class insignia, national letters and sail numbers shall when possible be wholly above an arc whose centre is the head point and whose radius is 60% of the leech length. They shall be placed at different heights on the two sides of the sail, those on the starboard side being uppermost.

(b) The class insignia shall be placed above the national letters. If the class insignia is of such a design that two of them coincide when placed back to back on both sides of the sail, they may be so placed.

(c) National letters shall be placed above the sail number.

(d) The national letters and sail number shall be displayed on the front side of a spinnaker but may be placed on both sides. They shall be displayed wholly below an arc whose centre is the head point and whose radius is 40% of the foot median and, when possible, wholly above an arc whose radius is 60% of the foot median.

(e) The national letters and sail number shall be displayed on both sides of a headsail whose clew can extend behind the mast 30% or more of the mainsail foot length. They shall be displayed wholly below an arc whose centre is the head point and whose radius is half the luff length and, if possible, wholly above an arc whose radius is 75% of the luff length.

G2 OTHER BOATS

Other boats shall comply with the rules of their national authority or class association in regard to the allotment, carrying and size of insignia, letters and numbers. Such rules shall, when practicable, conform to the above requirements.

US SAILING prescribes that, unless otherwise stated in her class rules, the sails of a boat that is not in an ISAF International Class or Recognized Class shall comply with rule G1. However, offshore racing boats not in a class that is subject to rule G1 shall carry numbers allotted by US SAILING on mainsails, spinnakers and each overlapping headsail having a luff-perpendicular measurement exceeding 130% of the base of the foretriangle. This rule applies only to boats whose owners' national authority is US SAILING. See www.ussailing.org/rules/sailnumbers for the full text of the Sail Numbering System for offshore racing boats in the United States and for an application for a sail number.

G3   CHARTERED OR LOANED BOATS

When so stated in the notice of race or sailing instructions, a boat chartered or loaned for an event may carry national letters or a sail number in contravention of her class rules.

G4   WARNINGS AND PENALTIES

When a protest committee finds that a boat has broken a rule of this appendix it shall either warn her and give her time to comply or penalize her.

G5   CHANGES BY CLASS RULES

ISAF classes may change the rules of this appendix provided the changes have first been approved by the ISAF.

Appendix H — Weighing Clothing and Equipment

See rule 43. This appendix shall not be changed by sailing instructions or prescriptions of national authorities.

H1 Items of clothing and equipment to be weighed shall be arranged on a rack. After being saturated in water the items shall be allowed to drain freely for one minute before being weighed. The rack must allow the items to hang as they would hang from clothes hangers, so as to allow the water to drain freely. Pockets that have drain-holes that cannot be closed shall be empty, but pockets or items that can hold water shall be full.

H2 When the weight recorded exceeds the amount permitted, the competitor may rearrange the items on the rack and the equipment inspector or measurer shall again soak and weigh them. This procedure may be repeated a second time if the weight still exceeds the amount permitted.

H3 A competitor wearing a dry suit may choose an alternative means of weighing the items.
   (a) The dry suit and items of clothing and equipment that are worn outside the dry suit shall be weighed as described above.
   (b) Clothing worn underneath the dry suit shall be weighed as worn while *racing*, without draining.
   (c) The two weights shall be added together.

Appendix J — Notice of Race and Sailing Instructions

See rules 89.2(a) and 90.2. The term 'race' includes a regatta or other series of races.

J1 NOTICE OF RACE CONTENTS

J1.1 The notice of race shall include the following information:

(1) the title, place and dates of the race and name of the organizing authority;

(2) that the race will be governed by the *rules* as defined in *The Racing Rules of Sailing*;

(3) a list of any other documents that will govern the event (for example, *The Equipment Rules of Sailing*, to the extent that they apply), stating where or how each document or a copy of it may be seen;

(4) the classes to race, any handicap or rating system that will be used and the classes to which it will apply, conditions of entry and any restrictions on entries;

(5) the times of registration and warning signals for the practice race, if one is scheduled, and the first race, and succeeding races if known.

J1.2 The notice of race shall include any of the following that will apply and that would help competitors decide whether to attend the event or that conveys other information they will need before the sailing instructions become available:

(1) identification of any racing rules that will be changed, a summary of the changes, and a statement that the changes will appear in full in the sailing instructions (see rule 86);

(2) that advertising will be restricted to Category A or that boats will be required to display advertising chosen and supplied by the organizing authority (see ISAF Regulation 20) and other information related to Regulation 20;

(3) any classification requirements that some or all competitors must satisfy (see rule 79 and ISAF Regulation 22, Sailor Classification Code);

(4) for an event where entries from other countries are expected, any national prescriptions that may require advance preparation;

(5) the procedure for advance registration or entry, including fees and any closing dates;

(6) an entry form, to be signed by the boat's owner or owner's representative, containing words such as 'I agree to be bound by *The Racing Rules of Sailing* and by all other *rules* that govern this event.';

(7) equipment inspection, measurement procedures or requirements for measurement certificates or for handicap or rating certificates;

(8) the time and place at which the sailing instructions will be available;

(9) changes to class rules, as permitted under rule 87, referring specifically to each rule and stating the change;

(10) the courses to be sailed;

(11) the penalty for breaking a rule of Part 2, other than the Two-Turns Penalty;

(12) denial of the right of appeal, subject to rule 70.5;

(13) the scoring system, if different from the Low Point System in Appendix A, the number of races scheduled and the minimum number that must be completed to constitute a series;

(14) prizes.

J2 SAILING INSTRUCTION CONTENTS

J2.1 The sailing instructions shall include the following information:

(1) that the race will be governed by the *rules* as defined in *The Racing Rules of Sailing*;

(2) a list of any other documents that will govern the event (for example, *The Equipment Rules of Sailing*, to the extent that they apply);

(3) the schedule of races, the classes to race and times of warning signals for each class;

(4) the course(s) to be sailed, or a list of *marks* from which the course will be selected and, if relevant, how courses will be signalled;

(5) descriptions of *marks*, including starting and finishing *marks*, stating the order and side on which each is to be left and identifying all rounding *marks* (see rule 28.1);

(6) descriptions of the starting and finishing lines, class flags and any special signals to be used;

(7) the time limit, if any, for *finishing*;

(8) the handicap or rating system to be used, if any, and the classes to which it will apply;

      (9) the scoring system, if different from the Low Point System in Appendix A, included by reference to Appendix A, to class rules or other *rules* governing the event, or stated in full. State the number of races scheduled and the minimum number that must be completed to constitute a series.

J2.2 The sailing instructions shall include those of the following that will apply:

      (1) that advertising will be restricted to Category A (see ISAF Regulation 20) and other information related to Regulation 20;

      (2) replacement of the rules of Part 2 with the right-of-way rules of the *International Regulations for Preventing Collisions at Sea* or other government right-of-way rules, the time(s) or place(s) they will apply, and any night signals to be used by the race committee;

      (3) changes to the racing rules permitted by rule 86, referring specifically to each rule and stating the change (if rule 86.2 applies, state the authorization);

      (4) changes to the national prescriptions (see rule 88);

      (5) when appropriate, at an event where entries from other countries are expected, a copy in English of the national prescriptions that will apply;

      (6) changes to class rules, as permitted under rule 87, referring specifically to each rule and stating the change;

      (7) restrictions controlling changes to boats when supplied by the organizing authority;

      (8) the registration procedure;

      (9) measurement or inspection procedure;

   (10) location(s) of official notice board(s);

   (11) procedure for changing the sailing instructions;

   (12) safety requirements, such as requirements and sig-nals for personal flotation devices, check-in at the starting area, and check-out and check-in ashore;

   (13) declaration requirements;

   (14) signals to be made ashore and location of signal station(s);

   (15) the racing area (a chart is recommended);

   (16) approximate course length and approximate length of windward legs;

(17) description of any area designated by the race committee to be an *obstruction* (see the definition *Obstruction*);

(18) the time limit, if any, for the first boat to *finish* and the time limit, if any, for boats other than the first boat to *finish*;

(19) time allowances;

(20) the location of the starting area and any restrictions on entering it;

(21) any special procedures or signals for individual or general recall;

(22) boats identifying *mark* locations;

(23) any special procedures or signals for changing a leg of the course (see rule 33);

(24) any special procedures for shortening the course or for *finishing* a shortened course;

(25) restrictions on use of support boats, plastic pools, radios, etc.; on trash disposal; on hauling out; and on outside assistance provided to a boat that is not *racing*;

(26) the penalty for breaking a rule of Part 2, other than the Two-Turns Penalty;

(27) under rule 86.1(b), a change to the number of hull lengths determining the *zone*;

(28) whether rule 67 or Appendix P will apply;

(29) protest procedure and times and place of hearings;

(30) if rule N1.4(b) will apply, the time limit for requesting a hearing under that rule;

(31) when required by rule 70.3, the national authority to which appeals and requests may be sent and, when applicable, subject to rule 70.5 denial of the right of appeal;

(32) the national authority's approval of the appointment of an international jury, when required under rule 91(b);

(33) substitution of competitors;

(34) the minimum number of boats appearing in the starting area required for a race to be started;

(35) when and where races *postponed* or *abandoned* for the day will be resailed;

(36) tides and currents;

(37) prizes;

(38) other commitments of the race committee and obligations of boats.

Appendix K — Notice of Race Guide

This guide provides a notice of race designed primarily for major championship regattas for one or more classes. It therefore will be particularly useful for world, continental and national championships and other events of similar importance. It can be downloaded from the ISAF website (www.sailing.org) as a basic text for producing a notice of race for any particular event.

The guide can also be useful for other events. However, for such events some of the paragraphs will be unnecessary or undesirable. Organizing authorities should therefore be careful in making their choices.

This guide relates closely to Appendix L, Sailing Instructions Guide, and its expanded version Appendix LE on the ISAF website, the introduction to which contains principles that also apply to a notice of race.

To use this guide, first review rule J1 and decide which paragraphs will be needed. Paragraphs that are required by rule J1.1 are marked with an asterisk (*). Delete all inapplicable or unnecessary paragraphs. Select the version preferred where there is a choice. Follow the directions in the left margin to fill in the spaces where a solid line (_____) appears and select the preferred wording if a choice or option is shown in brackets ([...]).

After deleting unused paragraphs, renumber all paragraphs in sequential order. Be sure that paragraph numbers are correct where one paragraph refers to another.

The items listed below, when applicable, should be distributed with the notice of race, but should not be included as numbered paragraphs in the notice.

1   An entry form, to be signed by the boat's owner or owner's representative, containing words such as 'I agree to be bound by The Racing Rules of Sailing *and by all other rules that govern this event.'*

2   For an event where entries from other countries are expected, the applicable national prescriptions in English.

3   List of sponsors, if appropriate.

4   Lodging and camping information.

5   Description of meal facilities.

6   *Race committee and protest committee members.*

7   *Special mooring or storage requirements.*

8   *Sail and boat repair facilities and ship's chandlers.*

9   *Charter boat availability.*

On separate lines, insert the full name of the regatta, the inclusive dates from measurement or the practice race until the final race or closing ceremony, the name of the organizing authority, and the city and country.

_____

_____

_____

_____

_____

_____

_____

NOTICE OF RACE

1   RULES

1.1*   The regatta will be governed by the rules as defined in *The Racing Rules of Sailing.*

Use the first sentence if appropriate. Insert the name. List by number and title the prescriptions that will not apply (see rule 88).Use the second sentence if it applies and if entries from other countries are expected, and state the relevant prescriptions in full.

1.2   [The following prescriptions of the _____ national authority will not apply: _____.] [The prescriptions that may require advance preparation are stated in full below.]

(OR)

Use only if the national authority for the venue of the event has not adopted a prescription to rule 88.

1.2   No national prescriptions will apply.

List by name any other documents that govern the event; for example, The Equipment Rules of Sailing, *to the extent that they apply.*	**1.3***	_____ will apply.
See rule 86. Insert the rule number(s) and summarize the changes.	**1.4**	Racing rule(s) _____ will be changed as follows: _____. The changes will appear in full in the sailing instructions. The sailing instructions may also change other racing rules.
Insert the rule number(s) and class name. Make a separate statement for the rules of each class.	**1.5**	Under rule 87, rule(s) _____ of the _____ class rules [will not apply] [is (are) changed as follows: ___].
	1.6	If there is a conflict between languages the English text will take precedence.

2   ADVERTISING

See ISAF Regulation 20. Include other applicable information related to Regulation 20.	**2.1**	Advertising will be restricted to Category A.
See ISAF Regulation 20.3(d).	**2.2**	Boats may be required to display advertising chosen and supplied by the organizing authority.

3*   ELIGIBILITY AND ENTRY

Insert the class(es).	**3.1**	The regatta is open to all boats of the _____ class(es).
	(OR)	
Insert the class(es) and eligibility requirements.	**3.1**	The regatta is open to boats of the _____ class(es) that _____.
Insert the postal, fax and e-mail addresses and entry closing date.	**3.2**	Eligible boats may enter by completing the attached form and sending it, together with the required fee, to _____ by _____.
Insert any conditions.	**3.3**	Late entries will be accepted under the following conditions: _____.

Insert any restrictions.	**3.4**	The following restrictions on the number of boats apply: ____.

4   CLASSIFICATION

Insert any requirements.   The following classification requirements will apply (see rule 79):

____.

5   FEES

Insert all required fees   **5.1** Required fees are as follows:
for racing.

Class	Fee
_____	_____
_____	_____
_____	_____

Insert optional fees   **5.2** Other fees:
(for example, for social
events).   _____

_____

**6   QUALIFYING SERIES AND
FINAL SERIES**

Use only when a class is   The regatta will consist of a
divided into fleets racing   qualifying series and a final series.
a qualifying series and
a final series.

7   SCHEDULE

Insert the day, date   **7.1*** Registration:
and times.

Day and date _____

From _____ To _____

Insert the day, date   **7.2** Measurement and inspection:
and times.

Day and date _____

From _____ To _____

Revise as desired and in-   **7.3*** Dates of racing:
sert the dates and classes.
Include a practice race if
any. When the series con-
sists of qualifying races
and final races, specify
them. The schedule can
also be given in an
attachment.

Date	Class _____	Class _____
_____	racing	racing
_____	racing	reserve day
_____	reserve day	racing
_____	racing	racing
_____	racing	racing

Insert the classes and numbers.	**7.4**	Number of races:

Class	Number	Races per day
——	——	——
——	——	——
——	——	——

Insert the time.

7.5* The scheduled time of the warning signal for the [practice race] [first race] [each day] is ____.

8   MEASUREMENTS

List the measurements with appropriate references to the class rules.

Each boat shall produce a valid [measurement] [rating] certificate.

(OR)

Each boat shall produce a valid [measurement] [rating] certificate. In addition the following measurements [may] [will] be taken: ____.

9   SAILING INSTRUCTIONS

Insert the time, date and location.

The sailing instructions will be available after ____ on ____ at ____.

10   VENUE

Insert a number or letter. Provide a marked map with driving instructions.

10.1 Attachment ____ shows the location of the regatta harbour.

Insert a number or letter. Provide a marked map or chart.

10.2 Attachment ____ shows the location of the racing areas.

11   THE COURSES

Include the description.

The courses to be sailed will be as follows: ____.

(OR)

Insert a number or letter. A method of illustrating various courses is shown in Addendum A of Appendix L or LE. Insert the course length if applicable.

The diagrams in Attachment ____ show the courses, including the approximate angles between legs, the order in which marks are to be passed, and the side on which each mark is to be left. [The approximate course length will be ____.]

12   PENALTY SYSTEM

Include paragraph 12.1 only when the Two-Turns Penalty will not be used. Insert the number of places or describe the penalties.

12.1 The Scoring Penalty, rule 44.3, will apply. The penalty will be _____ places.

(OR)

12.1 The penalties are as follows: _____.

Insert the class(es).

12.2 For the _____ class(es) rule 44.1 is changed so that the Two-Turns Penalty is replaced by the One-Turn Penalty.

Include only if the protest committee is an international jury or another provision of rule 70.5 applies. Use 'jury' only if referring to an international jury.

12.3 Decisions of the [protest committee] [jury] will be final as provided in rule 70.5.

13   SCORING

Include only if the Low Point System is replaced by the Bonus Point System.

13.1 The Bonus Point System of Appendix A will apply.

(OR)

Include only if neither of the Appendix A scoring systems will be used. Describe the system.

13.1 The scoring system is as follows: _____.

Insert the number.

13.2 _____ races are required to be completed to constitute a series.

Insert the numbers throughout.

13.3 (a) When fewer than _____ races have been completed, a boat's series score will be the total of her race scores.

(b) When from _____ to _____ races have been completed, a boat's series score will be the total of her race scores excluding her worst score.

(c) When _____ or more races have been completed, a

boat's series score will be
the total of her race scores
excluding her two worst
scores.

14   SUPPORT BOATS

*Insert the identification
markings. National let-
ters are suggested for
international events.*

Support boats shall be marked
with _____.

15   BERTHING

Boats shall be kept in their
assigned places in the [boat
park] [harbour].

16   HAUL-OUT RESTRICTIONS

Keelboats shall not be hauled out
during the regatta except with
and according to the terms of
prior written permission of the
race committee.

**17   DIVING EQUIPMENT AND
     PLASTIC POOLS**

Underwater breathing apparatus
and plastic pools or their equivalent shall not be used around
keelboats between the preparatory signal of the first race and
the end of the regatta.

18   RADIO COMMUNICATION

*Insert any alternative text
that applies. Describe the
radio communication
bands or frequencies
that will be used or
allowed.*

Except in an emergency, a boat
shall neither make radio transmissions while racing nor receive
radio communications not available to all boats. This restriction
also applies to mobile telephones.

19   PRIZES

*If perpetual trophies will
be awarded state their
complete names.*

Prizes will be given as follows:
_____.

The laws applicable to the venue in which the event is held may limit disclaimers. Any disclaimer should be drafted to comply with those laws.

20 DISCLAIMER OF LIABILITY

Competitors participate in the regatta entirely at their own risk. See rule 4, Decision to Race. The organizing authority will not accept any liability for material damage or personal injury or death sustained in conjunction with or prior to, during, or after the regatta.

21 INSURANCE

Insert the currency and amount.

Each participating boat shall be insured with valid third-party liability insurance with a minimum cover of _____ per event or the equivalent.

22 FURTHER INFORMATION

Insert necessary contact information.

For further information please contact _____.

Appendix L — Sailing Instructions Guide

This guide provides a set of tested sailing instructions designed primarily for major championship regattas for one or more classes. It therefore will be particularly useful for world, continental and national championships and other events of similar importance. The guide can also be useful for other events; however, for such events some of these instructions will be unnecessary or undesirable. Race officers should therefore be careful in making their choices.

An expanded version of the guide, Appendix LE, is available on the ISAF website (www.sailing.org). It contains provisions applicable to the largest and most complicated multi-class events, as well as variations on several of the sailing instructions recommended in this appendix. It will be revised from time to time, to reflect advances in race management techniques as they develop, and can be downloaded as a basic text for producing the sailing instructions for any particular event. Appendix L can also be downloaded from the ISAF website.

The principles on which all sailing instructions should be based are as follows:

1   *They should include only two types of statement: the intentions of the race committee and protest committee and the obligations of competitors.*
2   *They should be concerned only with racing. Information about social events, assignment of moorings, etc., should be provided separately.*
3   *They should not change the racing rules except when clearly desirable. (When they do so, they must follow rule 86 by referring specifically to the rule being changed and stating the change.)*
4   *They should not repeat or restate any of the racing rules.*
5   *They should not repeat themselves.*
6   *They should be in chronological order; that is, the order in which the competitor will use them.*
7   *They should, when possible, use words or phrases from the racing rules.*

To use this guide, first review rule J2 and decide which instructions will be needed. Instructions that are required by rule J2.1 are marked with an asterisk (*). Delete all *inapplicable or unnecessary instructions. Select the version preferred where there is a choice. Follow the directions in the left margin to fill in the spaces where a solid line (_____) appears and select the preferred wording if a choice or option is shown in brackets ([. . .]).*

After deleting unused instructions, renumber all instructions in sequential order. Be sure that instruction numbers are correct where one instruction refers to another.

***US SAILING Note:** US SAILING has produced a guide to simplified sailing instructions suitable for events such as club or local regattas. This guide can be found at www.ussailing.org/rules/simpleSIs.*

On separate lines, insert the full name of the regatta, the inclusive dates from measurement or the practice race until the final race or closing ceremony, the name of the organizing authority, and the city and country.

_____

_____

_____

_____

_____

_____

_____

SAILING INSTRUCTIONS

1 RULES

1.1* The regatta will be governed by the rules as defined in *The Racing Rules of Sailing*.

Use the first sentence if appropriate. Insert the name. List by number and title the prescriptions that will not apply (see rule 88). Use the second sentence if it applies and if entries from other national authorities are expected, and state the prescriptions in full.

1.2 [The following prescriptions of the _____ national authority will not apply: _____.] [The prescriptions hat will apply are stated in full below.]

(OR)

Use only if the national authority for the venue of the event has not adopted a prescription to rule 88.

1.2 No national prescriptions will apply.

List by name any other documents that govern the event; for example, The Equipment Rules of Sailing, *to the extent that they apply.*

1.3* _____ will apply.

See rule 86. Either insert here the rule number(s) and state the changes, or, if not using this instruction, do the same in each instruction that changes a rule.

1.4 Racing rule(s) _____ will be changed as follows: _____.

For example, use 'two' when the racing area is particularly small or 'four' when the boats are particularly fast.

1.5 Under rule 86.1(b), in the definition Zone the distance is changed to [two] [four] hull lengths.

Insert the rule number(s) and class name. Make a separate statement for the rules of each class.

1.6 Under rule 87, rule(s) _____ of the _____ class rules [will not apply] [is (are) changed as follows: ___].

1.7 If there is a conflict between languages the English text will take precedence.

2 NOTICES TO COMPETITORS

Insert the location(s).

Notices to competitors will be posted on the official notice board(s) located at _____.

3 CHANGES TO SAILING INSTRUCTIONS

Change the times if different.

Any change to the sailing instructions will be posted before 0900 on the day it will take effect, except that any change to the schedule of races will be posted by 2000 on the day before it will take effect.

4   SIGNALS MADE ASHORE

Insert the location.

4.1 Signals made ashore will be displayed at ＿＿＿.

Insert the number of minutes.

4.2 When flag AP is displayed ashore, '1 minute' is replaced with 'not less than ＿＿＿ minutes' in the race signal AP.

(OR)

Insert the number of minutes.

4.2 Flag D with one sound means 'The warning signal will be made not less than ＿＿＿ minutes after flag D is displayed. [Boats are requested not to leave the harbour until this signal is made.]'

Delete if covered by a class rule.

4.3 When flag Y is displayed ashore, rule 40 applies at all times while afloat. This changes the Part 4 preamble.

5   SCHEDULE OF RACES

Revise as desired and insert the dates and classes. Include a practice race if any. When the series consists of qualifying races and final races, specify them. The schedule can also be given in an attachment.

5.1* Dates of racing:

Date	Class ＿＿＿	Class ＿＿＿
＿＿＿	racing	racing
＿＿＿	racing	reserve day
＿＿＿	reserve day	racing
＿＿＿	racing	racing
＿＿＿	racing	racing

Insert the classes and numbers.

5.2* Number of races:

Class	Number	Races per day
＿＿＿	＿＿＿	＿＿＿
＿＿＿	＿＿＿	＿＿＿

One extra race per day may be sailed, provided that no class becomes more than one race ahead of schedule and the change is made according to instruction 3.

Insert the time.

5.3* The scheduled time of the warning signal for the first race each day is ＿＿＿.

5.4 After a long postponement, to alert boats that a race or sequence of races will begin soon, an orange flag will be displayed with one sound for at least four minutes before a warning signal is displayed.

Insert the time.

5.5 On the last day of the regatta no warning signal will be made after _____.

6* **CLASS FLAGS**

Insert the classes and names or descriptions of the flags.

Class flags will be:

Class	Flag

7 **RACING AREAS**

Insert a number or letter.

Attachment _____ shows the location of racing areas.

8 **THE COURSES**

Insert a number or letter. A method of illustrating various courses is shown in Addendum A. Insert the course length if applicable.

8.1* The diagrams in Attachment _____ show the courses, including the approximate angles between legs, the order in which marks are to be passed, and the side on which each mark is to be left. [The approximate course length will be _____.]

8.2 No later than the warning signal, the race committee signal boat will display the approximate compass bearing of the first leg.

8.3 Courses will not be shortened. This changes rule 32.

Include only when changing positions of marks is impracticable.

8.4 Legs of the course will not be changed after the preparatory signal. This changes rule 33.

9 MARKS

Change the mark numbers as needed and insert the descriptions of the marks. Use the second alternative when Marks 4S and 4P form a gate, with Mark 4S to be left to starboard and Mark 4P to port.

9.1* Marks 1, 2, 3 and 4 will be _____.

(OR)

9.1* Marks 1, 2, 3, 4S and 4P will be _____.

Unless it is clear from the course diagrams, list the marks that are rounding marks.

9.2 The following marks are rounding marks: _____.

Insert the descriptions of the marks.

9.3 New marks, as provided in instruction 12.1, will be _____.

Describe the starting and finishing marks: for example, the race committee signal boat at the starboard end and a buoy at the port end. Instruction 11.2 will describe the starting line and instruction 13 the finishing line.

9.4* The starting and finishing marks will be _____.

9.5 A race committee boat signalling a change of a leg of the course is a mark as provided in instruction 12.2.

10 AREAS THAT ARE OBSTRUCTIONS

Describe each area by its location and any easily recognized details of appearance.

The following areas are designated as obstructions: _____.

11 THE START

Include only if the asterisked option in rule 26 will be used. Insert the number of minutes.

11.1 Races will be started by using rule 26 with the warning signal made _____ minutes before the starting signal.

(OR)

Describe any starting system other than that stated in rule 26.

11.1 Races will be started as follows: _____. This changes rule 26.

11.2* The starting line will be between staffs displaying orange flags on the starting marks.

(OR)

11.2* The starting line will be between a staff displaying an orange flag on the starting mark at the starboard end and the port-end starting mark.

(OR)

Insert the description.

11.2* The starting line will be _____.

11.3 Boats whose warning signal has not been made shall avoid the starting area during the starting sequence for other races.

Insert the number of minutes.

11.4 A boat starting later than _____ minutes after her starting signal will be scored Did Not Start without a hearing. This changes rules A4 and A5.

Insert the channel number.

11.5 If any part of a boat's hull, crew or equipment is on the course side of the starting line during the two minutes before her starting signal and she is identified, the race committee will attempt to broadcast her sail number on VHF channel _____. Failure to make a broadcast or to time it accurately will not be grounds for a request for redress. This changes rule 62.1(a).

12 **CHANGE OF THE NEXT LEG OF THE COURSE**

12.1 To change the next leg of the course, the race committee will move the original mark (or the finishing line) to a new position.

(OR)

12.1 To change the next leg of the course, the race committee will lay a new mark (or move the finishing line) and remove the original mark as soon as practicable. When in a subsequent change a new mark is replaced, it will be replaced by an original mark.

Reverse 'port' and 'star-board' when the mark is to be left to starboard.

12.2 Except at a gate, boats shall pass between the race committee boat signalling the change of the next leg and the nearby mark, leaving the mark to port and the race committee boat to starboard. This changes rule 28.1.

This is a US SAILING prescription.

12.3 *If the race committee intends to start another race on the same day, it will display the Second Substitute (with no sound) while boats are finishing.*

13* THE FINISH

The finishing line will be between staffs displaying orange flags on the finishing marks.

(OR)

The finishing line will be between a staff displaying an orange flag on the finishing mark at the star-board end and the port-end finishing mark.

(OR)

Insert the description.

The finishing line will be _____.

14   PENALTY SYSTEM

Include instruction 14.1 only when the Two-Turns Penalty will not be used.

14.1 The Scoring Penalty, rule 44.3, will apply. The penalty will be _____ places.

(OR)

Insert the number of places or describe the penalties.

14.1 The penalties are as follows:
_____.

Insert the class(es).

14.2 For the _____ class(es) rule 44.1 is changed so that the Two-Turns Penalty is replaced by the One-Turn Penalty.

Here and below, use 'jury' only when referring to an international jury.

14.3 As provided in rule 67, the [protest committee] [jury] may, without a hearing, penalize a boat that has broken rule 42.

(OR)

Unless all of Appendix P applies, state any restrictions.

14.3 Appendix P will apply [as changed by instruction(s) [14.2] [and] [14.4]].

Recommended only for junior events.

14.4 Rule P2.3 will not apply and rule P2.2 is changed so that it will apply to any penalty after the first one.

15   TIME LIMITS AND TARGET TIMES

Insert the classes and times. Omit the Mark 1 time limit and target time if inapplicable.

15.1* Time limits and target times are as follows:

Class	Time limit	Mark 1 time limit	Target time
_____	_____	_____	_____
_____	_____	_____	_____
_____	_____	_____	_____

If no boat has passed Mark 1 within the Mark 1 time limit the race will be abandoned. Failure to meet the target time will not be grounds for redress. This changes rule 62.1(a).

Insert the time (or different times for different classes).

15.2 Boats failing to finish within _____ after the first boat sails the course and finishes will be scored Did Not Finish without a hearing. This changes rules 35, A4 and A5.

16 PROTESTS AND REQUESTS FOR REDRESS

State the location if necessary.

16.1 Protest forms are available at the race office[, located at _____]. Protests and requests for redress or reopening shall be delivered there within the appropriate time limit.

Change the time if different.

16.2 For each class, the protest time limit is 90 minutes after the last boat has finished the last race of the day.

Change the posting time if different. Insert the protest room location and, if applicable, the time for the first hearing.

16.3 Notices will be posted no later than 30 minutes after the protest time limit to inform competitors of hearings in which they are parties or named as witnesses. Hearings will be held in the protest room, located at _____, beginning at [the time posted] [_____].

16.4 Notices of protests by the race committee or [protest committee] [jury] will be posted to inform boats under rule 61.1(b).

16.5 A list of boats that, under instruction 14.3, have been penalized for breaking rule 42 will be posted.

16.6 Breaches of instructions 11.3, 18, 21, 23, 24, 25, 26 and 27 will not be grounds for a protest by a boat. This changes rule 60.1(a). Penalties for these breaches may be less than disqualification if the [protest committee] [jury] so decides. The scoring abbreviation for a discretionary penalty imposed under this instruction will be DPI.

16.7 On the last scheduled day of racing a request for reopening a hearing shall be delivered

(a) within the protest time limit if the requesting party was informed of the decision on the previous day;

Change the time if different.

(b) no later than 30 minutes after the requesting party was informed of the decision on that day.

This changes rule 66.

16.8 On the last scheduled day of racing a request for redress based on a [protest committee] [jury] decision shall be delivered no later than 30 minutes after the decision was posted. This changes rule 62.2.

Include only if the protest committee is an international jury or another provision of rule 70.5 applies.

16.9 Decisions of the [protest committee] [jury] will be final as provided in rule 70.5.

This is a US SAILING prescription.

16.10 *If the race committee posts a list of boats scored OCS, ZFP or BFD on the official notice board before the protest time limit, a request for redress based on such a posted score shall be made no later than one hour after the protest time limit. This changes the first sentence of rule 62.2.*

17   SCORING

Include only if the Low Point System is replaced by the Bonus Point System.

17.1* The Bonus Point System of Appendix A will apply.

(OR)

Include only if neither of the Appendix A scoring systems will be used. Describe the system.

17.1* The scoring system is as follows: _____.

Insert the number.

17.2* _____ races are required to be completed to constitute a series.

Insert the numbers throughout.

17.3 (a) When fewer than _____ races have been completed, a boat's series score will be the total of her race scores.

(b) When from _____ to _____ races have been completed, a boat's series score will be the total of her race scores excluding her worst score.

(c) When _____ or more races have been completed, a boat's series score will be the total of her race scores excluding her two worst scores.

18   SAFETY REGULATIONS

Insert the procedure for check-out and check-in.

18.1 Check-Out and Check-In: _____.

18.2 A boat that retires from a race shall notify the race committee as soon as possible.

19   REPLACEMENT OF CREW OR EQUIPMENT

19.1 Substitution of competitors will not be allowed without prior written approval of the [race committee] [protest committee] [jury].

19.2 Substitution of damaged or lost equipment will not be allowed unless authorized by the [race committee] [protest committee] [jury]. Requests for substitution shall be made to the committee at the first reasonable opportunity.

20   EQUIPMENT AND MEASUREMENT CHECKS

A boat or equipment may be inspected at any time for compliance with the class rules and sailing instructions. On the water, a boat can be instructed by a race committee equipment inspector or measurer to proceed immediately to a designated area for inspection.

21   ADVERTISING

See ISAF Regulation 20.3(d). Insert necessary information on the advertising material.

Boats [shall] [may] display advertising supplied by the organizing authority as follows: _____.

22   OFFICIAL BOATS

Insert the descriptions. If appropriate, use different identification markings for boats performing different duties.

Official boats will be marked as follows: _____.

23   SUPPORT BOATS

23.1 Team leaders, coaches and other support personnel shall stay outside areas where boats are racing from the time of the preparatory signal for the first class to start until all boats have finished or retired or the race committee signals a postponement, general recall or abandonment.

Insert the identification markings. National letters are suggested for international events.

23.2 Support boats shall be marked with _____.

24   TRASH DISPOSAL

Boats shall not put trash in the water. Trash may be placed aboard support and race committee boats.

25 HAUL-OUT RESTRICTIONS

Keelboats shall not be hauled out during the regatta except with and according to the terms of prior written permission of the race committee.

26 DIVING EQUIPMENT AND PLASTIC POOLS

Underwater breathing apparatus and plastic pools or their equivalent shall not be used around keel boats between the preparatory signal of the first race and the end of the regatta.

27 RADIO COMMUNICATION

Insert any alternative text that applies. Describe the radio communication bands or frequencies that will be used or allowed.

Except in an emergency, a boat shall neither make radio transmissions while racing nor receive radio communications not available to all boats. This restriction also applies to mobile telephones.

28 PRIZES

If perpetual trophies will be awarded state their complete names.

Prizes will be given as follows: _____.

29 DISCLAIMER OF LIABILITY

The laws applicable to the venue in which the event is held may limit disclaimers. Any disclaimer should be drafted to comply with those laws.

Competitors participate in the regatta entirely at their own risk. See rule 4, Decision to Race. The organizing authority will not accept any liability for material damage or personal injury or death sustained in conjunction with or prior to, during, or after the regatta.

30 INSURANCE

Insert the currency and amount.

Each participating boat shall be insured with valid third-party liability insurance with a minimum cover of _____ per event or the equivalent.

ADDENDUM A — ILLUSTRATING THE COURSE

Shown here are diagrams of course shapes. The boat's track is represented by a discontinuous line so that each diagram can describe courses with different numbers of laps. If more than one course may be used for a class, state how each particular course will be signalled.

A Windward-Leeward Course

Start – 1 – 2 – 1 – 2 – Finish

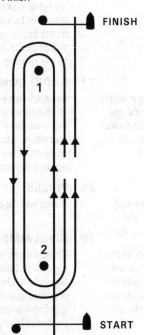

Options for this course include

(1)   *increasing or decreasing the number of laps,*

(2)   *deleting the last windward leg,*

(3)   *using a gate instead of a leeward mark,*

(4)   *using an offset mark at the windward mark, and*

(5)   *using the leeward and windward marks as starting and finishing marks.*

A Windward-Leeward-Triangle Course

Start – 1 – 2 – 3 – 1 – 3 – Finish

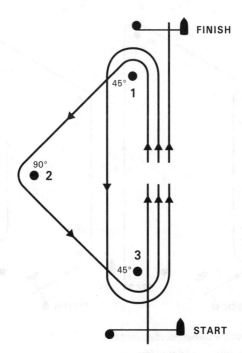

Options for this course include

(1)   increasing or decreasing the number of laps,

(2)   deleting the last windward leg,

(3)   varying the interior angles of the triangle
(45°–90°–45° and 60°–60°–60° are common),

(4)   using a gate instead of a leeward mark for downwind legs,

(5)   using an offset mark at the beginning of downwind legs, and

(6)   using the leeward and windward marks as starting and
finishing marks.

Be sure to specify the interior angle at each mark.

Trapezoid Courses

Start – 1 – 2 – 3 – 2 – 3 – Finish   Start – 1 – 4 – 1 – 2 – 3 – Finish

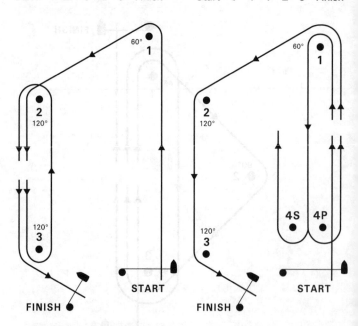

Options for these courses include

(1)   adding additional legs,

(2)   replacing the gate shown by a single mark, or using a gate also in the outer loop,

(3)   varying the interior angles of the reaching legs,

(4)   using an offset mark at the beginning of downwind legs, and

(5)   finishing boats upwind rather than on a reach.

Be sure to specify the interior angle of each reaching leg.

ADDENDUM B — BOATS PROVIDED BY THE ORGANIZING AUTHORITY

The following sailing instruction is recommended when all boats will be provided by the organizing authority. It can be changed to suit the circumstances. When used, it should be inserted after instruction 3.

4   BOATS

4.1   Boats will be provided for all competitors, who shall not modify them or cause them to be modified in any way except that

(a)   a compass may be tied or taped to the hull or spars;

(b)   wind indicators, including yarn or thread, may be tied or taped anywhere on the boat;

(c)   hulls, centreboards and rudders may be cleaned, but only with water;

(d)   adhesive tape may be used anywhere above the water line; and

(e)   all fittings or equipment designed to be adjusted may be adjusted, provided that the class rules are complied with.

4.2   All equipment provided with the boat for sailing purposes shall be in the boat while afloat.

4.3   The penalty for not complying with one of the above instructions will be disqualification from all races sailed in which the instruction was broken.

4.4   Competitors shall report any damage or loss of equipment, however slight, to the organizing authority's representative immediately after securing the boat ashore. The penalty for breaking this instruction, unless the [protest committee] [jury] is satisfied that the competitor made a determined effort to comply, will be disqualification from the race most recently sailed.

4.5   Class rules requiring competitors to be members of the class association will not apply.

Appendix M — Recommendations for Protest Committees

This appendix is advisory only; in some circumstances changing these procedures may be advisable. It is addressed primarily to protest committee chairmen but may also help judges, protest committee secretaries, race committees and others connected with protest and redress hearings.

In a protest or redress hearing, the protest committee should weigh all testimony with equal care; should recognize that honest testimony can vary, and even be in conflict, as a result of different observations and recollections; should resolve such differences as best it can; should recognize that no boat or competitor is guilty until a breach of a *rule* has been established to the satisfaction of the protest committee; and should keep an open mind until all the evidence has been heard as to whether a boat or competitor has broken a *rule*.

M1 PRELIMINARIES
(may be performed by race office staff)
- Receive the *protest* or request for redress.
- Note on the form the time the *protest* or request is delivered and the protest time limit.
- Inform each *party*, and the race committee when necessary, when and where the hearing will be held.

M2 BEFORE THE HEARING
Make sure that
- each *party* has a copy of or the opportunity to read the *protest* or request for redress and has had reasonable time to prepare for the hearing.
- no member of the protest committee is an *interested party*. Ask the *parties* whether they object to any member. When redress is requested under rule 62.1(a), a member of the race committee should not be a member of the protest committee.
- only one person from each boat (or *party*) is present unless an interpreter is needed.
- all boats and people involved are represented. If they are not, however, the committee may proceed under rule 63.3(b).

- boats' representatives were on board when required (rule 63.3(a)). When the *parties* were in different races, both organizing authorities must accept the composition of the protest committee (rule 63.8). In a measurement *protest* obtain the current class rules and identify the authority responsible for interpreting them (rule 64.3(b)).

M3   THE HEARING

M3.1 Check the validity of the *protest* or request for redress.

- Are the contents adequate (rule 61.2 or 62.1)?
- Was it delivered in time? If not, is there good reason to extend the time limit (rule 61.3 or 62.2)?
- When required, was the protestor involved in or a witness to the incident (rule 60.1(a))?
- When necessary, was 'Protest' hailed and, if required, a red flag displayed correctly (rule 61.1(a))?
- When the flag or hail was not necessary, was the protestee informed?
- Decide whether the *protest* or request for redress is valid (rule 63.5).
- Once the validity of the *protest* or request has been determined, do not let the subject be introduced again unless truly new evidence is available.

M3.2 Take the evidence (rule 63.6).

- Ask the protestor and then the protestee to tell their stories. Then allow them to question one another. In a redress matter, ask the *party* to state the request.
- Invite questions from protest committee members.
- Make sure you know what facts each *party* is alleging before calling any witnesses. Their stories may be different.
- Allow anyone, including a boat's crew, to give evidence. It is the *party* who normally decides which witnesses to call, although the protest committee may also call witnesses (rule 63.6). The question asked by a *party* 'Would you like to hear N?' is best answered by 'It is your choice.'
- Call each *party's* witnesses (and the protest committee's if any) one by one. Limit *parties* to questioning the witness(es) (they may wander into general statements).

123

- Invite the protestee to question the protestor's witness first (and vice versa). This prevents the protestor from leading his witness from the beginning.
- Allow a member of the protest committee who saw the incident to give evidence (rule 63.6) but only in the presence of the *parties*. The member may be questioned and may remain in the room (rule 63.3(a)).
- Try to prevent leading questions or hearsay evidence, but if that is impossible discount the evidence so obtained.
- Accept written evidence from a witness who is not available to be questioned only if all *parties* agree. In doing so they forego their rights to question that witness (rule 63.6).
- Ask one member of the committee to note down evidence, particularly times, distances, speeds, etc.
- Invite first the protestor and then the protestee to make a final statement of her case, particularly on any application or interpretation of the *rules*.

M3.3 Find the facts (rule 63.6).

- Write down the facts; resolve doubts one way or the other.
- Call back *parties* for more questions if necessary.
- When appropriate, draw a diagram of the incident using the facts you have found.

M3.4 Decide the *protest* or request for redress (rule 64).

- Base the decision on the facts found (if you cannot, find some more facts).
- In redress cases, make sure that no further evidence is needed from boats that will be affected by the decision.

M3.5 Inform the *parties* (rule 65).

- Recall the *parties* and read them the facts found, conclusions and *rules* that apply, and the decision. When time presses it is permissible to read the decision and give the details later.
- Give any *party* a copy of the decision on request. File the *protest* or request for redress with the committee records.

M4   REOPENING A HEARING (rule 66)

When a *party*, within the time limit, has asked for a hearing to be reopened, hear the *party* making the request, look at any video, etc., and decide whether there is any material new evidence that might lead you to change your decision. Decide whether your interpretation of the *rules* may have been wrong; be open-minded as to whether you have made a mistake. If none of these applies refuse to reopen; otherwise schedule a hearing.

M5   GROSS MISCONDUCT (rule 69)

M5.1 An action under this rule is not a *protest,* but the protest committee gives its allegations in writing to the competitor before the hearing. The hearing is conducted under the same rules as other hearings but the protest committee must have at least three members (rule 69.1(b)). Use the greatest care to protect the competitor's rights.

M5.2 A competitor or a boat cannot protest under rule 69, but the protest form of a competitor who tries to do so may be accepted as a report to the protest committee, which can then decide whether or not to call a hearing.

M5.3 When it is desirable to call a hearing under rule 69 as a result of a Part 2 incident, it is important to hear any boat-vs.-boat *protest* in the normal way, deciding which boat, if any, broke which *rule*, before proceeding against the competitor under this rule.

M5.4 Although action under rule 69 is taken against a competitor, not a boat, a boat may also be penalized (rule 69.1(b)).

M5.5 The protest committee may warn the competitor (rule 69.1(b)(1)), in which case no report is to be made (rule 69.1(c)). When a penalty is imposed and a report is made as required by rule 69.1(c) or 69.1(e), it may be helpful to recommend whether or not further action should be taken.

M6   APPEALS (rule 70 and Appendix F)

When decisions can be appealed,

- retain the papers relevant to the hearing so that the information can easily be used for an appeal. Is there a diagram endorsed or prepared by the protest committee?

Are the facts found sufficient? (Example: Was there an *overlap*? Yes or No. 'Perhaps' is not a fact found.) Are the names of the protest committee members and other important information on the form?

- comments by the protest committee on any appeal should enable the appeals committee to picture the whole incident clearly; the appeals committee knows nothing about the situation.

M7 PHOTOGRAPHIC EVIDENCE

Photographs and videotapes can sometimes provide useful evidence but protest committees should recognize their limitations and note the following points:

- The *party* producing the photographic evidence is responsible for arranging the viewing.
- View the tape several times to extract all the information from it.
- The depth perception of any single-lens camera is very poor; with a telephoto lens it is non-existent. When the camera views two *overlapped* boats at right angles to their course, it is impossible to assess the distance between them. When the camera views them head on, it is impossible to see whether an *overlap* exists unless it is substantial.
- Ask the following questions:
  - Where was the camera in relation to the boats?
  - Was the camera's platform moving? If so in what direction and how fast?
  - Is the angle changing as the boats approach the critical point? Fast panning causes radical change.
  - Did the camera have an unrestricted view throughout?

Appendix N — International Juries

See rules 70.5 and 91(b). This appendix shall not be changed by sailing instructions or national prescriptions.

N1 COMPOSITION, APPOINTMENT AND ORGANIZATION

N1.1 An international jury shall be composed of experienced sailors with excellent knowledge of the racing rules and extensive protest committee experience. It shall be independent of and have no members from the race committee, and be appointed by the organizing authority, subject to approval by the national authority if required (see rule 91(b)), or by the ISAF under rule 89.2(b).

N1.2 The jury shall consist of a chairman, a vice chairman if desired, and other members for a total of at least five. A majority shall be International Judges. The jury may appoint a secretary, who shall not be a member of the jury.

N1.3 No more than two members (three, in Groups M, N and Q) shall be from the same national authority.

N1.4 (a) The chairman of a jury may appoint one or more panels composed in compliance with rules N1.1, N1.2 and N1.3. This can be done even if the full jury is not composed in compliance with these rules.

   (b) The chairman of a jury of fewer than ten members may appoint two or three panels of at least three members each, of which the majority shall be International Judges. Members of each panel shall be from at least three different national authorities except in Groups M, N and Q, where they shall be from at least two different national authorities. If dissatisfied with a panel's decision, a *party* is entitled to a hearing by a panel composed in compliance with rules N1.1, N1.2 and N1.3, except concerning the facts found, if requested within the time limit specified in the sailing instructions.

N1.5 When a full jury, or a panel, has fewer than five members, because of illness or emergency, and no qualified replacements are available, it remains properly constituted if it consists of at least three members and if at least two of them are International Judges. When there are three or four members they shall be from at least three different national authorities except in Groups M, N and Q, where they shall be from at least two different national authorities.

N1.6 When the national authority's approval is required for the appointment of an international jury (see rule 91(b)), notice of its approval shall be included in the sailing instructions or be posted on the official notice board.

N1.7 If the jury or a panel acts while not properly constituted, its decisions may be appealed.

N2 RESPONSIBILITIES

N2.1 An international jury is responsible for hearing and deciding all *protests*, requests for redress and other matters arising under the rules of Part 5. When asked by the organizing authority or the race committee, it shall advise and assist them on any matter directly affecting the fairness of the competition.

N2.2 Unless the organizing authority directs otherwise, the jury shall decide

    (a) questions of eligibility, measurement or boat certificates; and

    (b) whether to authorize the substitution of competitors, boats or equipment when a *rule* requires such a decision.

N2.3 The jury shall also decide matters referred to it by the organizing authority or the race committee.

N3 PROCEDURES

N3.1 Decisions of the jury, or of a panel, shall be made by a simple majority vote of all members. When there is an equal division of votes cast, the chairman of the meeting may cast an additional vote.

N3.2 When it is considered desirable that some members not participate in discussing and deciding a *protest* or request for redress, and no qualified replacements are available, the jury or panel remains properly constituted if at least three members remain and at least two of them are International Judges.

N3.3 Members shall not be regarded as *interested parties* (see rule 63.4) by reason of their nationality.

N3.4 If a panel fails to agree on a decision it may adjourn, in which case the chairman shall refer the matter to a properly constituted panel with as many members as possible, which may be the full jury.

Appendix P — Special Procedures for Rule 42

All or part of this appendix applies only if the sailing instructions so state.

P1 SIGNALLING A PENALTY

A member of the protest committee or its designated observer who sees a boat breaking rule 42 may penalize her by, as soon as reasonably possible, making a sound signal, pointing a yellow flag at her and hailing her sail number, even if she is no longer *racing*. A boat so penalized shall not be penalized a second time under rule 42 for the same incident.

P2 PENALTIES

P2.1 First Penalty

When a boat is first penalized under rule P1 her penalty shall be a Two-Turns Penalty under rule 44.2. If she fails to take it she shall be disqualified without a hearing.

P2.2 Second Penalty

When a boat is penalized a second time during the regatta, her penalty shall be to promptly retire from the race. If she fails to take it she shall be disqualified without a hearing and her score shall not be excluded.

P2.3 Third and Subsequent Penalties

When a boat is penalized a third or subsequent time during the regatta, she shall promptly retire from the race. If she does so her penalty shall be disqualification without a hearing and her score shall not be excluded. If she fails to do so her penalty shall be disqualification without a hearing from all races in the regatta, with no score excluded, and the protest committee shall consider calling a hearing under rule 69.1(a).

P3 POSTPONEMENT, GENERAL RECALL OR ABANDONMENT

If a boat has been penalized under rule P1 and the race committee signals a *postponement*, general recall or *abandonment*, the penalty is cancelled, but it is still counted to determine the number of times she has been penalized during the regatta.

P4   REDRESS LIMITATION

A boat shall not be given redress for an action by a member of the protest committee or its designated observer under rule P1 unless the action was improper due to a failure to take into account a race committee signal or a class rule.

P5   FLAGS O AND R

(a) If the class rules permit pumping, rocking and ooching when the wind speed exceeds a specified limit, the race committee may signal that those actions are permitted, as specified in the class rules, by displaying flag O before or with the warning signal. The flag shall be removed at the starting signal.

(b) If the wind speed exceeds the specified limit after the starting signal, the race committee may display flag O with repetitive sounds at a *mark* to signal to a boat that the actions are permitted, as specified in the class rules, after she has passed the *mark*.

(c) If the wind speed becomes less than the specified limit after flag O was displayed, the race committee may display flag R with repetitive sounds at a *mark* to signal to a boat that rule 42, as changed by the class rules, applies after she has passed the *mark*.

Appendix S — Sound-Signal Starting System

This appendix is a US SAILING prescription.
US SAILING prescribes that, when the sailing instructions so indicate, the Sound-Signal Starting System described below shall be used. This system is recommended primarily for small-boat racing and makes it unnecessary for competitors to use stopwatches. Supplemental visual course and recall signals are also recommended when practicable.

S1 Course and postponement signals may be made orally.

S2 Audible signals shall govern, even when supplemental visual signals are also used.

S3 The starting sequence shall consist of the following sound signals made at the indicated times:

Signal	Sound	Time before start
Warning	3 long	3 minutes
Preparatory	2 long	2 minutes
	1 long, 3 short	1 minute, 30 seconds
	1 long	1 minute
	3 short	30 seconds
	2 short	20 seconds
	1 short	10 seconds
	1 short	5 seconds
	1 short	4 seconds
	1 short	3 seconds
	1 short	2 seconds
	1 short	1 second
Starting	1 long	0

S4 Signals shall be timed from their commencement.

S5 A series of short signals may be made before the sequence begins in order to attract attention.

S6 Individual recalls shall be signalled by the hail of the sail number (or some other clearly distinguishing feature) of each recalled boat. Flag X need not be displayed.

S7 Failure of a competitor to hear an adequate course, postponement, starting sequence or recall signal shall not be grounds for redress.

Protest Form

SAILING. also for requests for redress and reopening

| Date & time received |
| Received by _____ Filing no. _____ |

1. **EVENT** _____ Organizing authority _____ Date ____ Race no. ____

2. **TYPE OF HEARING**

   ☐ Protest by boat against boat

   ☐ Protest by race committee against boat

   ☐ Protest by protest committee against boat

   ☐ Request for redress by boat or race committee

   ☐ Consideration of redress by protest committee

   ☐ Request by boat or race committee to reopen hearing

   ☐ Consideration of reopening by protest committee

3. **BOAT PROTESTING, OR REQUESTING REDRESS OR REOPENING**

   Class _____ Sail no. _____ Boat's name _____

   Represented by _____ Tel. _____ E-mail _____

4. **BOAT(S) PROTESTED OR BEING CONSIDERED FOR REDRESS**

   Class _____ Sail no. _____ Boat's name _____

5. **INCIDENT**

   Time and place of incident _____

   Rule(s) alleged to have been broken _____ Witness(es) _____

6. **INFORMING PROTESTEE**

   How did you inform the protestee of your intention to protest?

   ☐ By hailing When? _____ Word(s) used _____

   ☐ By displaying a red flag When? _____

   ☐ By informing her in some other way Give details _____

7. **DESCRIPTION OF INCIDENT**
   (use another sheet if necessary)

   Diagram: one square = one hull length
   Show position of boats, wind
   and current direction, marks.

❏ Withdrawal requested; signature_____ ❏ Withdrawal permitted

Protest time limit _____ ❏ Protest, or request for redress or ❏ Time limit extended
reopening, received within time limit

Protestor, or party requesting redress or reopening, represented by _____

Other party, or boat being considered for redress, represented by _____

Names of witnesses _____

Interpreters _____   **Remarks**

No objection about interested party . . . . ❏ _____

Written protest or request identifies incident . . . ❏ _____

'Protest' hailed at first reasonable opportunity . . ❏ _____

No hail needed; protestee informed at first . . . . . ❏ _____
reasonable opportunity

Red flag conspicuously displayed at first . . . . ❏ _____
reasonable opportunity

❏ **Protest or request valid; hearing will continue**   ❏ **Protest or request invalid;
hearing is closed**

FACTS FOUND

❏ Diagram of boat ___ is endorsed by committee. ❏ Committee's diagram is attached.

CONCLUSIONS AND RULES THAT APPLY

DECISION

Protest: ❏ dismissed   Boat(s)_____ is (are)   ❏ disqualified from race(s)_____
                                                     ❏ penalized as follows _____

Redress: ❏ not given   ❏ given as follows_____

Request to reopen a hearing: ❏ denied ❏ granted	**Written decision requested**
PROTEST COMMITTEE	When _____
Members _____	By whom _____
Chairman's signature _____ Date & time _____	Date provided _____

Index

References are to rule numbers (for example, 27.3), appendices and their rule numbers (for example, C or E3.10), and sections of the book (for example, Introduction, Race Signals). Defined terms appear in *italics*. Appendices K, L and M are not indexed except for their titles. ***US SAILING prescriptions are not included in the Index.***

Definitions

*A term used as stated below is shown in italic type or, in preambles, in **bold italic** type.*

Abandon A race that a race committee or protest committee *abandons* is void but may be resailed.

Clear Astern** and **Clear Ahead**; **Overlap One boat is *clear astern* of another when her hull and equipment in normal position are behind a line abeam from the aftermost point of the other boat's hull and equipment in normal position. The other boat is *clear ahead*. They *overlap* when neither is *clear astern*. However, they also *overlap* when a boat between them *overlaps* both. These terms always apply to boats on the same *tack*. They do not apply to boats on opposite *tacks* unless rule 18 applies or both boats are sailing more than ninety degrees from the true wind.

Fetching A boat is *fetching* a *mark* when she is in a position to pass to windward of it and leave it on the required side without changing *tack*.

Finish A boat *finishes* when any part of her hull, or crew or equipment in normal position, crosses the finishing line in the direction of the course from the last *mark*, either for the first time or after taking a penalty under rule 44.2 or, after correcting an error made at the finishing line, under rule 28.1.

Interested Party A person who may gain or lose as a result of a protest committee's decision, or who has a close personal interest in the decision.

Keep Clear One boat *keeps clear* of another if the other can sail her course with no need to take avoiding action and, when the boats are *overlapped* on the same *tack*, if the *leeward* boat can change course in both directions without immediately making contact with the *windward* boat.

Leeward** and **Windward A boat's *leeward* side is the side that is or, when she is head to wind, was away from the wind. However, when sailing by the lee or directly downwind, her *leeward* side is the side on which her mainsail lies. The other side is her *windward* side. When two boats on the same *tack overlap*, the one on the *leeward* side of the other is the *leeward* boat. The other is the *windward* boat.

Mark An object the sailing instructions require a boat to leave on a specified side, and a race committee boat surrounded by navigable water from which the starting or finishing line extends. An anchor line or an object attached temporarily or accidentally to a *mark* is not part of it.

Mark-Room *Room* for a boat to sail to the *mark*, and then *room* to sail her *proper course* while at the *mark*. However, *mark-room* does not include *room* to tack unless the boat is *overlapped* to *windward* and on the inside of the boat required to give *mark-room*.

Obstruction An object that a boat could not pass without changing course substantially, if she were sailing directly towards it and one of her hull lengths from it. An object that can be safely passed on only one side and an area so designated by the sailing instructions are also *obstructions*. However, a boat *racing* is not an *obstruction* to other boats unless they are required to *keep clear* of her, give her *room* or *mark-room* or, if rule 22 applies, avoid her. A vessel under way, including a boat *racing*, is never a continuing *obstruction*.

Overlap See **Clear Astern** and **Clear Ahead**; **Overlap**.

Party A *party* to a hearing: a protestor; a protestee; a boat requesting redress; a boat or a competitor that may be penalized under rule 69.1; a race committee or an organizing authority in a hearing under rule 62.1(a).

Postpone A *postponed* race is delayed before its scheduled start but may be started or *abandoned* later.

Proper Course A course a boat would sail to *finish* as soon as possible in the absence of the other boats referred to in the rule using the term. A boat has no *proper course* before her starting signal.

Protest An allegation made under rule 61.2 by a boat, a race committee or a protest committee that a boat has broken a *rule*.

Racing A boat is *racing* from her preparatory signal until she *finishes* and clears the finishing line and *marks* or retires, or until the race committee signals a general recall, *postponement* or *abandonment*.

Room The space a boat needs in the existing conditions while manoeuvring promptly in a seamanlike way.

Rule (a) The rules in this book, including the Definitions, Race Signals, Introduction, preambles and the rules of relevant appendices, but not titles;

(b) ISAF Regulation 19, Eligibility Code; Regulation 20, Advertising Code; Regulation 21, Anti-Doping Code; and Regulation 22, Sailor Classification Code;

(c) the prescriptions of the national authority, unless they are changed by the sailing instructions in compliance with the national authority's prescription, if any, to rule 88;

(d) the class rules (for a boat racing under a handicap or rating system, the rules of that system are 'class rules');

(e) the notice of race;

(f) the sailing instructions; and

(g) any other documents that govern the event.

Start A boat *starts* when, having been entirely on the pre-start side of the starting line at or after her starting signal, and having complied with rule 30.1 if it applies, any part of her hull, crew or equipment crosses the starting line in the direction of the first *mark*.

Tack, Starboard* or *Port A boat is on the *tack*, *starboard* or *port*, corresponding to her *windward* side.

Windward See ***Leeward* and *Windward***.

Zone The area around a *mark* within a distance of three hull lengths of the boat nearer to it. A boat is in the *zone* when any part of her hull is in the *zone*.

Sail fast,
sail fair.